Disinherited Generations

Disinherited Generations

Our Struggle to Reclaim Treaty Rights
for First Nations Women and their Descendants

NELLIE CARLSON &

KATHLEEN STEINHAUER

as told to LINDA GOYETTE

THE UNIVERSITY OF ALBERTA PRESS

Published by

The University of Alberta Press
Ring House 2
Edmonton, Alberta, Canada T6G 2E1
www.uap.ualberta.ca

LIBRARY AND ARCHIVES CANADA
CATALOGUING IN PUBLICATION

Carlson, Nellie
    Disinherited generations : our struggle
to reclaim treaty rights for First Nations
women and their descendants / Nellie
Carlson & Kathleen Steinhauer ; as told
to Linda Goyette.

Includes bibliographical references and index.
Issued also in electronic formats.
ISBN 978-0-88864-642-2

    1. Carlson, Nellie. 2. Steinhauer,
Kathleen. 3. Native activists—Canada—
Biography. 4. Native women—Canada—
Biography. 5. Women human rights
workers—Canada—Biography. 6. Cree
women—Canada—Biography. 7. Native
women—Legal status, laws, etc.—Canada.
8. Native peoples—Legal status, laws, etc.—
Canada. 9. Oral history—Canada.
I. Steinhauer, Kathleen II. Goyette, Linda,
1955– III. Title.

E78.C2C367 2013   323.1197´07100922
C2012-908030-6

First edition, second printing, 2014.
Printed and bound in Canada by Houghton
Boston Printers, Saskatoon, Saskatchewan.
Photo scanning by Dave Vasicek, Colorspace.
Copyediting and proofreading by
Peter Midgley.
Indexing by Judy Dunlop.

The University of Alberta Press is committed
to protecting our natural environment.
As part of our efforts, this book is printed
on Enviro Paper: it contains 100% post-
consumer recycled fibres and is acid- and
chlorine-free.

The University of Alberta Press gratefully acknowledges the support received for
its publishing program from The Canada
Council for the Arts. The University of
Alberta Press also gratefully acknowledges
the financial support of the Government
of Canada through the Canada Book Fund
(CBF) and the Government of Alberta
through the Alberta Multimedia Development
Fund (AMDF) for its publishing activities.

Canadä   Canada Council   Conseil des Arts
           for the Arts   du Canada

Government
of Alberta ■

To the children of the First Nations—all of them

We made history. It was thought at one time that it could never be done, but we did it.

—NELLIE CARLSON

I made the snowballs, and Nellie threw them.

—KATHLEEN STEINHAUER

Contents

otôtêmitowak/they are friends

 **Foreword**

A Tribute to Kathleen Steinhauer and Nellie Carlson

MARIA CAMPBELL

I ARRIVED IN EDMONTON IN 1963, not wanting to go "home" to Saskatchewan because there was nothing there for me or my three small children. I liked the small town feeling; it was friendly and I heard people speaking my language on the streets. I rented a small house on the South Side and in a short time I became part of a warm, supportive native community. That community was made up of Gilbert Anderson, Kathleen Steinhauer, Nellie Carlson, Jenny Margetts, Stan Daniels, Harold Cardinal, Eugene Steinhauer, Alex Janvier and many, many more. "Urban Aboriginal people," we say today, but back then our differences were not as important as they later became. What stands out for me when I think back was the sense of community we had and although many of us were from different parts of the country, our native roots bound us together and the differences that were important and often hurtful at home, were the things that brought us together in the city.

We had all in various ways, and for various reasons, been displaced from our families and communities. The Edmonton community of the early 1960s was made up of Halfbreeds, who were the Cree/English/Scot mixed bloods; the Métis, who were Cree/French; treaty Indians who had status cards and came from nearby Indian reserves; and non-status Indians whose families had not been present at the treaty-making process or for various other reasons had been dis-enfranchised. An example of this dis-enfranchisement was Kathleen's husband, Gilbert Anderson, whose community, the Michel First Nation, just a few miles outside of Edmonton, had been enfranchised in 1958. Gilbert was an Indian who, through no fault of his own, became a non-status Indian. Other people were non-status because they had joined the army or had gone to university, or their fathers or grandfathers had voluntarily given up their Indian status and in so doing had disinherited their descendants. Then there were the people like Kathleen and Nellie who were treaty Indians but who had lost their status when they married non-status Indians, Métis or Whitemen. Kathleen married Gilbert, a non-status Indian, and lost her status.

These differences were never understood by outsiders who didn't care anyway—we were all just "Indians or Breeds" to them and I do not believe any of them ever gave much thought to our language, or to our cultural or tribal differences and they certainly knew nothing about our history or the policies and legislation that had been passed by the federal government so it could have easy access to our lands.

I first saw Kathleen at a community dance sponsored by the Canadian Native Friendship Centre. I remember thinking "Oh my goodness, who is that elegant woman." Her mother was a Scot, her father a Cree Indian who was also the chief of her reserve. She was tall, slim, fair-haired with hazel eyes and had the most amazing laugh. And as I learned once I got to know her, an equally amazing sense of humour. We didn't meet that night, but several days later my good friend Gilbert Anderson phoned and said he was coming over for coffee and he was also bringing someone with him. Expecting him to arrive with another friend of ours, I was surprised to see him with the woman from the dance. She was as lovely as she looked and very funny. We had a great visit. As they were leaving, Gilbert announced that they were getting married and asked whether I would come to the wedding. They were married in 1965 and Kathleen and I became great friends. I don't believe we ever, in all the years we knew each other, went a week without visiting—whether it was in person or by phone. She was a kind, loving and fierce woman who, as Linda Goyette wrote in her eulogy, "never backed down from a bully in her life, not even when that bully was the Government of Canada."

I met Jenny Margetts at a women's gathering at the Friendship Centre about the same time I met Kathleen. I don't remember much about the meeting but I do remember how smart she was and that she knew how to organize. I learned that she had become a nun to get a higher education, later leaving the convent to marry and raise a family. She was a solid woman, not crazy humorous like Kathleen but more serious and business-like.

And Nellie I first heard at a meeting, ripping into somebody. When I saw her I was amazed. She was a tiny woman, almost like a little bird, fiery and not afraid to stand up and be heard. Her Cree was impeccable. It didn't matter how challenging something was, if Nellie focused on it she would not let it go. She was tenacious and courageous, reminding me of my grannies—if you were going into her kitchen you had better know what you were doing and know the escape route because she did not suffer fools gladly.

These three women were all related and came from the same reserve. All of them had lost their treaty status when they married. Kathleen and Nellie to non-status Indians and Jenny to a Whiteman. In Edmonton they organized cultural events, community dances and events for kids, working closely with the "old ladies" at the Friendship Centre. These old ladies were in their seventies and eighties and were the heart of the Friendship Centre movement. Younger women like Kathleen and many others were their helpers.

As a result of their collective hard work, Edmonton had a strong cohesive Aboriginal community.

These women were also the first generation of women that I knew of who had left residential school and went on to get careers. Kathleen was a public health nurse; Jenny trained as a teacher, and also worked as a business manager. Nellie, who was older, didn't have the same opportunities but that didn't stop her involvement in anything. She was always supportive of young people and encouraged everyone to get as much education as possible. Nellie still does this today by working as an elder with youth in community schools. The women were also well read and had a good understanding of history and colonization. They understood the Department of Indian Affairs and its policies and legislation better, I am sure, than most chiefs and band councils. And each of them married kind, respectful, hardworking and supportive men and they raised good families.

So we had a thriving native community in Edmonton, but about the mid-1960s things started to change. Political organizations emerged and within a few years it was like something shattered. Community activities did not stop, but the politics created difference and then when government funding came in, the community was fractured. All of a sudden it was important that we were treaty or Métis. Non-status Indians could join forces with Métis or be left out in the cold. At a meeting in Edmonton one day, a decision was made that all mixed bloods would become Métis and the word Halfbreed would no longer be recognized or used. Then there were the women like Kathleen, Jenny and Nellie who had lost status but were not prepared to give it up. They were Indians who had been left an inheritance of status through treaty. It was their right and they would pass it on to their children, government or no government.

They did not start the movement to organize for Indian Rights for Indian Women, but they had been thinking and stewing about it for a long time and when they heard about the Corbière Lavell case in Ontario, and the organizing work of Mary Two-Axe Earley in Quebec, they decided to get involved by forming an Ad Hoc Committee. They

moved effortlessly from cultural and social organizing to fighting for
rights, seeing no difference in the struggle to reclaim culture and the
struggle to regain their rights and the rights of their children.

Their work to preserve the inheritance of their children and to
begin mending *wâhkôhtowina*, was the beginning of real healing for
our people. When they said "no more," those brave words opened
the door for others to speak about the hidden pain and horrors of
childhood when there was no one to say "no more."

Their leadership style was unique. Their strategy was to host
small meetings, spread the word, and women and some men came.
They kept people informed. They had very little money to work with.
At first it was their family allowances, small donations, husbands
who paid the phone bills, and later small grants from the Secretary
of State. Most, if not all, of the consulting and legal work done, to my
knowledge, was pro bono.

They faced a lot of backlash from their own people. They were
insulted, ridiculed and humiliated. They were called "Squaw Libbers"
and threatened with beatings and threats that they and their families would be shot if they tried coming back to their reserves. Where
does this meanness come from? We need to think on this, as this is
the kind of violent thinking that will destroy us, not our blood being
thinned out.

Credit is given or taken today by many people for the success of
the struggle to regain lost Indian status, and many of the people who
take credit actually worked against them. If we are ever to stop the
violence perpetrated against Aboriginal women and their families in
this country, it is imperative that we look critically and also from a
cultural lens at the policies and legislation that have been passed by
the Canadian and provincial governments. Policies and legislation
that are, at their core, misogynistic, and have long-term effects. Land
claims are important, as are better housing, health and education,
but it is when we end the violence that we will create the real change.

Today when people talk about these rights they more often
than not say, "Yes but look what they did, they got status back for

themselves and their children and grandchildren. Soon the reserves will be filled with non-Indians." Well, that sounds to me like they are saying, "Indian is not about culture, it is about status."

Nothing has ever been written about these women and the sacrifices they made. We know nothing about the humiliation they endured or the threats to their lives and the lives of their families. Threats made by their leadership and their people to stop their organizing all across this country. We know a little about the Corbière Lavell case but even that is not well documented and there is nothing written about them. Who were these women?

These were and are strong Native women, just like their *ôhkomiwâwa* and *ocâpâniwâwa*, who stayed strong, retained their faith, and kept their sense of humour. They were good women, the kind of warriors we need today. What can I say? I loved and admired them.

This is a small and modest book, just like Nellie and Kathleen. It does not try to be anything more, and it is about moms, aunties and *ninôhkominânak* fighting, as they have always done, for a good life for their children and families. The politics here is not the Ottawa kind so admired by patriarchal leadership. This book is about kitchen work, which in the end always gets finished and is what *pimâtisiwin* is really all about. I want to end this with a note to Nellie.

Dearest Nellie,

It is with great sadness that I write this. I had hoped it would be done before Kathleen passed away. I have always wanted to say thank you in a very public way. Not just to the two of you, but also to the women across Canada who walked with you. I never had the opportunity to do that until you and Kathleen asked me to write this foreword. I am not a First Nations woman although I received treaty status through marriage, a status I turned down. I could never justify accepting it when my grandmother lost hers to marry my Métis grandfather. Ironic when you know that her grandfather was a chief and signator of Treaty Six and her great-grandfather

was the head chief. My granny died at the age of ninety-seven, two
years before Bill C-31 became law in 1985. It was always her greatest
wish to be buried beside her parents on her reserve. She is buried
in a nearby white cemetery with people she does not know. Like
many other Métis and non-status Indians across Canada, many
of my family members were discriminated against by this misogyn-
istic law. They and their families were reinstated when you won
this fight. You gave so much—all of you—and the benefit to your
people, our people, for we are all relatives, has been immeasur-
able. Did you know that 170,000 First Nations people benefited
from your struggle to restore an inheritance that is about identity,
belonging and place? Ay-hay thank you for your strength, forti-
tude and love. Thank you for protecting the inheritance of the
children and beginning the work of mending wâhkôhtowina. Your
actions were the beginning of real healing for our people. It is your
courage that is the catalyst, which will one day end violence against
Aboriginal women.

With love and respect,

MARIA CAMPBELL
Gabriel's Crossing
Batoche, Saskatchewan
July 16, 2012

Acknowledgements

THIS BOOK WAS A LONG, LONG TIME IN THE MAKING. We are grateful for the patience and support of our families through all the years.

We owe a great debt to author and activist Maria Campbell who was the first to encourage Nellie Carlson and Kathleen Steinhauer to preserve and share their stories about the Indian Rights for Indian Women movement. Maria nurtured this plan from its first days, and encouraged us to work together until we had finished the book. She has been an inspiration.

Jenny Margetts died in 1991 after leading the western branch of Indian Rights for Indian Women for twenty-five years. A great friend and mentor, she was in many ways a silent author of this book, too. By the time of her death, she had assembled a large and valuable collection of documents about First Nations and Métis political and social organizations, and extensive files on the fight against gender discrimination in the *Indian Act*. Her husband, Gordon Margetts, made this collection available to us, and we are very grateful for his support in this project. As for Jenny, we could almost hear her whispering to us as we worked on the book.

We appreciate the considerable assistance of Dr. Brenda Macdougall, now at the University of Ottawa; we met her when she was on the faculty of the Department of Native Studies at the University of Saskatchewan. Dr. Macdougall and research assistant Omeasoo Butt indexed the Jenny Margetts Collection for the benefit of future researchers. Kendall Stavast, then a student in the Faculty of Native Studies at the University of Alberta, kindly assisted with archival research and the transcription of an interview with Jenny Margetts. We are also grateful to Laverne Bender for her transcription of lengthy interviews with Nellie Carlson in 2001.

Darrell Loyer, Kathleen's son-in-law, assisted us with extra genealogical research, explaining and charting the many family links between the two cousins from Saddle Lake. Shirley Waskewitch of Prince Albert, Saskatchewan also provided assistance on the kinship lines of Kehewin. Naomi McIlwraith offered her generous assistance with the written Cree in this text. We are grateful for all of this help.

Finally we would like to thank our good friends at the University of Alberta Press for their early interest in the publication of this book. Three academic readers suggested many important improvements to the first draft, and we are grateful for their careful reviews. We appreciate the hard work of Linda Cameron, Mary Lou Roy, Alan Brownoff, Cathie Crooks, Monika Igali, Judy Dunlop and Duncan Turner who all had an important role in the publication of the book. Most of all we owe a great debt to Senior Editor Peter Midgley who believes in the power of storytelling, and understands the importance of oral history in our culture. His expert guidance helped to shape this book, and to deliver it to readers. Thank you, Peter, for understanding the power and potential of first-person narratives like this one.

The three authors accept full responsibility for any errors found in this text.

Finally we are grateful to one another for our enduring friendship.

—NELLIE CARLSON, KATHLEEN STEINHAUER & LINDA GOYETTE

niciwâmiskwêmak / cousins

 **Introduction**

Two Strong Women Begin to Tell a Story

LINDA GOYETTE

THE CREE LANGUAGE has a word for welcome, *tawâw*, which creates
a place for you in a warm and comfortable home. Come in, it means.
There is room for you here.

Take a seat at the kitchen table. You are about to listen to a long
series of conversations between two elders who have been lifelong
activists for treaty and Aboriginal rights in Alberta, and for women's
equality rights in Canada. This is a spoken history in the oral tradition of Cree and Métis culture on the prairies. Nellie Carlson and
Kathleen Steinhauer take turns speaking. Sometimes they tell a
story at the same time, finishing one another's sentences as they've
done since they were young women in Saddle Lake. Often they interrupt one another to challenge an interpretation of the historic events
that shaped their lives, or to explain in exhaustive detail how one
person in Cree country is related to another person in Cree country.
You might say that intermingled Cree and Métis genealogy is their

punctuation. As they speak, it is always clear that they are *nici-wâmiskwêmak*, first cousins, old friends, allies for life.

Throughout their lives, Nellie and Kathleen have rejected the Canadian government's never-ending attempts to define, legislate, and restrict the identity of the First Nations, Métis and Inuit peoples. They believe the indigenous peoples of this continent have the moral and legal right to assert their own identity, in their own words, at their own time, without interference.

This is the story of a long battle. "We created an organization called Indian Rights for Indian Women," Nellie begins. "We made history when we challenged Section 12(1)(b)—the discriminatory section of the old *Indian Act*.[1] People now have to understand what we were doing, and they are not really thinking about how that law affected them. It affected most Aboriginal families across Canada: their sisters, mothers, aunts and cousins."

More than 162,000 First Nations citizens in Canada can thank Nellie and Kathleen—and many brave women like them—for the treaty and Aboriginal rights they reclaimed after Canada ended sexual discrimination in the *Indian Act* in 1985.[2] Twenty-seven years later, these men, women and children are still waiting for justice, and that's why the oral testimony of two outspoken elders is so important.

♦ Nellie Carlson is now eighty-five. Kathleen Steinhauer was eighty when she died suddenly of heart failure on March 4, 2012, shortly before the publication of this book. Long ago their good friend from Saskatchewan, the writer and activist Maria Campbell, encouraged them to assemble a history of the Indian Rights for Indian Women movement so that this important knowledge would be preserved. That's when they approached me and asked for my help. I had interviewed Nellie Carlson, Jenny Margetts and Mary Two-Axe Earley in 1978 when I was a young newspaper reporter at the *Ottawa Citizen*, and I continued to cover the Indian Rights for Indian Women movement when I moved to Alberta to write for the *Edmonton Journal*.

After I left the newspaper trade in 2001, I became their friend and slowpoke stenographer. At regular intervals over the past eleven years, we have met so that they could tell the story of their significant campaign to reclaim full treaty rights for disinherited First Nations citizens. Over time they expanded their project to tell the personal stories from their childhood, adolescence and young adulthood that shaped their political activism later in life.

Nellie and I deeply regret that Kathleen did not live long enough to see the result of her hard work in print. Shortly before her death, she spoke of her excitement about the project, and her hope that the book would assist young people in search of their indigenous identity.

The conversations reproduced in this book occurred between the fall of 2000 and the summer of 2011 in four places: at Kathleen's kitchen table in north Edmonton; at Nellie's kitchen table a few city blocks to the south; in a hospital room at the Royal Alexandra Hospital in downtown Edmonton where Kathleen was a patient, and in the Virginia Park Senior Citizens' Lodge where she moved in 2011.

All stories are told in circles, not in a straight line. They are told in casual sentences, not in cold statistics or calendar dates. To create this book, Nellie and Kathleen told many versions of the same story, in slightly different ways, in the dozens of conversations I later transcribed. It was their preference that I refer to them by their first names throughout the text. As you listen to the two women speak, I will be sitting beside you at the table, the silent one, scribbling in a notebook as my soup gets cold. "Eat! Eat!" Kathleen would remind me. "I will in a minute," I would reply. Sometimes I interrupted with a question about a confusing matter—oh, that bewildering *Indian Act*—but mostly I tried to stay quiet, scribbling into my notebook, as the two elders spoke.

I am aware that a transcriber shapes the story and becomes part of it as an invisible third author. As a former newspaper and magazine journalist, and later an oral history researcher, anthologist, author and editor, I have struggled for thirty years with the complex

Nellie Mildred Carlson and Kathleen Amelia Jean Steinhauer.

ethical issues at the heart of this kind of work. Finding authentic ways to share oral history and contemporary storytelling has been a lifelong interest and concern. In the end, I never believe I get it right.

Canada has a long history of as-told-to narratives of Indigenous history with First Nations speakers and non-Aboriginal writers or editors. Inevitable difficulties, distortions, omissions and ethical challenges surface in this retelling of oral history in printed books and articles. Who has the right to tell a life story? Who has the right to edit and abbreviate it? How can the reader hear the warm, original voice of the storyteller among lines of print on a cold page, or see the wider truth outside the margins of a printed photograph or a paragraph? Can a non-Cree journalist properly transcribe a story rooted in the experiences of Cree storytellers when she has grown up in a country that refuses to confront the historic injustices that Aboriginal peoples continue to endure? Can *any* outsider be trusted with the important life story of someone else? I first struggled with these important issues when I studied journalism at Carleton University in Ottawa in the early 1970s, and I have read widely since then to keep up to date with the evolving debate, current practice (and malpractice) of my profession, and First Nations and other oral history protocols. Nellie and Kathleen have experienced these problems firsthand in their relationships with contemporary media throughout their lives so we were able to talk about our approach to the book, and plan it.

The three of us tried hard to invent our own kind of collaboration: something that suits our different ways of looking at the world, and our friendship. For example, even though no money was exchanged for this work, and I did not apply for grants to subsidize it, the three of us signed a detailed contract in advance to outline our shared obligations and our common understanding of our goals. I am indebted to both principal authors for their infinite patience with me, and yet I realize that my limitations as a non-Cree transcriber and editor influenced the final text, and interfered with the storytelling. If I lived to be twice the age of Nellie and Kathleen, I could not learn enough about their lives and culture and challenges to do their project justice. There is so much I will never understand. We ask readers to consider this problem as they listen to the story. All three of us did the best we could.

The conversations in this book were not conventional interviews. I did not prepare a list of questions in advance to structure a chronological narrative. I made a conscious effort not to interrupt the speakers too often, and for once I was in no hurry to close my notebook and return to a newsroom. In the early stages of this project, I made audiotapes of the discussions but found that the two elders spoke more freely and naturally without a tape recorder on the kitchen table. Later I took detailed notes of our conversations, and once at home, transcribed both notebooks and tapes into new computer files. Often Nellie or Kathleen would phone me to add their second thoughts to an afternoon's conversation, and I'd take notes then, too. Then I tried to put together the scattered fragments of many stories into a single draft manuscript without interrupting the speakers in the text, or changing their words or meaning. I tried to reflect the natural flow of their storytelling in several early drafts of this book. Three academic reviewers who read an early version of the manuscript made many suggestions, including a request for more background material in this introduction to put the speakers' testimony in historical context.

Nellie and Kathleen, the two principal authors, reviewed several drafts, and made their own corrections until they were satisfied with this version of the story. They were sharp-eyed editors of my transcription work. The text travelled back and forth between us, and was circulated among their families. I encourage readers who want to see the original transcripts—and explore the comprehensive Indian Rights for Indian Women files that Jenny Margetts assembled before her death—to consult the full collection which Kathleen and Nellie have donated to the Provincial Archives of Alberta.

Each chapter opens with a background introduction to the topic of their conversation to clarify issues and timelines for readers. Then the two women begin the story in their own words, adding rich detail and context, abundant humour and their own strong viewpoints.

Readers unfamiliar with Canada's Aboriginal history may be confused when Nellie and Kathleen discuss the way the byzantine *Indian Act* disrupted the lives of First Nations women and their children. To help others find their way through the spider's web, they have tried to explain in simple language the meaning of expressions such as "status Indian," "registered Indian," "treaty Indian," "non-status Indian" and "Bill c-31 Indian"—the imposed labels that split family members with the same lineage into different legal categories, with different legal rights. The word "Indian" is no longer used much in Canada, except by First Nations people themselves in certain circumstances, and in the language of the federal *Indian Act*. I have prepared a glossary, *Terms Related to the Identity of Aboriginal Peoples in Canada*, and a timeline, *Membership Rights and First Nations Women in Canada*, at the back of the book for readers who find themselves in unknown territory.

Nellie and Kathleen want this book to be a helpful guide to students, researchers and other people in the community. The two elders had no intention of producing a standard academic text that examines all sides of a complex issue with a goal of objectivity. They are women with strong opinions. They set out to tell a story from their own unique perspectives, as they experienced it. They recognize their conversations here will provoke deeper questions and contentious debate. With that in mind I have included a select bibliography at the end of the book for further reading, and footnotes to offer background context and profiles of some of the people they mention.

Canadian lawyers, politicians, civil servants, constitutional experts, historians, political scientists and journalists debate the same issues in dialects of their own, usually at a convenient distance from the community. For Nellie and Kathleen, Aboriginal and treaty rights are a personal matter, a family inheritance, something precious passed down from one generation to the next. Over and over again, they told me: We are writing this book for the sake of the children who follow us.

♦ First and always Nellie Carlson and Kathleen Steinhauer identify with the *nêhiyawak*, people of the Cree Nation. They define Aboriginal rights as the sacred rights that all indigenous people inherited from ancestors who were the original occupants of North America before Europeans arrived on the continent. To them, this means the right to a fair share of the land and its natural resources, the right for Aboriginal people to govern themselves, to practice and pass on their spiritual and cultural beliefs without interference, to raise and educate their children in their own communities, and to speak their own language. Since 1982 the Aboriginal rights of the First Nations, Métis and Inuit peoples[3] have been recognized and guaranteed in Section 35 of Canada's Constitution, and endlessly debated, tested and interpreted in the courts of the nation.

Treaty rights are distinct from Aboriginal rights. When European newcomers arrived in mainland Canada, beginning in the early

1600s, they negotiated their relationships with the First Nations in a series of agreements. Formal treaties were not signed in all parts of Canada—not in British Columbia, for example—but certain First Nations signed eleven numbered treaties with the Crown between 1871 and 1921.

Born on the Canadian prairies, Kathleen and Nellie grew up in the heart of Treaty Six territory. This is where their allegiance lies, and their kinship. Plains Cree leaders of the North-West negotiated the terms of Treaty Six with representatives of Queen Victoria at Fort Carlton and Fort Pitt in August and September of 1876. Many Cree chiefs, interpreters and witnesses at the signing came from the region where Nellie and Kathleen were born. Nellie can trace her ancestry through direct family ties to two of these chiefs, Onchaminahos, or Little Hunter; and Pakan, known in English as James Seenum. Weekaskookeeseyin, or Sweetgrass, and Kehewin also negotiated for the western Cree at Fort Pitt, and these leaders also represented the women's ancestors. Some of the Cree who lived further west could not come to the treaty signing, so their leaders signed adhesions to Treaty Six at Fort Edmonton in 1877 and 1888. Kathleen is related through her marriage and her own ancestors to two of these chiefs: Papastayo, known on the treaty document as Papaschase, and Michel Callihoo.

Nellie and Kathleen ask readers to look deeply into the prairie treaties, to learn more about them and to protect them. They wonder how much western Canadians of all backgrounds know about the promises in these documents. Treaty rights involve so much more than a treaty card in a wallet. In the historic written document of Treaty Six the Crown promised one square mile of land for each family of five, or about 128 acres per capita, in a permanent reserve; hunting and fishing rights; farming implements and seeds; rations during times of famine; a school, later interpreted as education benefits; a medicine chest, later interpreted as health care; and annual treaty payments of twenty-five dollars for the chief, and five dollars for each member.

However, the larger negotiations in Treaty Six involved the future of 313,400 square kilometres of traditional territory.

Like their families, and many Cree people, Nellie and Kathleen interpret Treaty Six as an enduring peace agreement between the First Nations and the British Crown. The federal government contends it was an agreement between the First Nations and the Government of Canada, a new nation at the time of the treaty signing. The written version of Treaty Six prepared by the Crown's representatives includes a promise that the First Nations would "cede, release surrender and yield up...all rights, titles and privileges" to a massive region of what is now central Alberta and Saskatchewan. According to Cree oral history, which Kathleen and Nellie accept, the chiefs and their descendants understood the treaty as an agreement to share the land and natural resources with newcomers for mutual benefit—not to surrender it altogether, or to place themselves under permanent authority of the Canadian government.

The *Indian Act* does not deliver treaty or Aboriginal rights. Introduced in 1876, it is one of the country's oldest enduring statutes. As far as Nellie and Kathleen are concerned, the Parliament of Canada invented this piece of legislation to control and sometimes eliminate the inherited rights that First Nations citizens claim as their own. "The *Indian Act* was their way to confuse the First Peoples in this certain way about the land they stole," says Nellie. Not only does the *Indian Act* say how reserves must be governed, which bands can be recognized, and what band councils can do, it also defines who can be recognized as "a status Indian" or a "treaty Indian"—a First Nations citizen with registered Indian legal status in the opinion of the state.

In the days before the *Indian Act*, Aboriginal peoples across the plains identified the members of their own bands. They often adopted children or invited adults from other tribal groups to join them in many different circumstances. Women moved between communities, as men did, and were accepted as members of their adopted community. Nellie points to Cree history in Alberta for evidence. "The Cree leader Bobtail, Kiskayo, had eight daughters," she said. "Every daughter married someone from a different reserve." Similarly, as a young man, the Plains Cree chief Poundmaker (Pîhtokahânapiwiyin) became the adopted son of Siksika chief Crowfoot (Isapo-Muxika), the head chief of the Blackfoot. Crowfoot had lost a son in 1873 during a raid on a Cree camp. Later one of his wives saw Poundmaker and was struck by his resemblance to the lost son. Crowfoot immediately adopted the young man, gave him a Blackfoot name, and invited him to remain for a time in his camp. Moving from community to community was a cultural tradition of the Cree people. After marriage, it was often traditional for a husband to move to the community of his wife's family.

Soon a bewildering set of government rules interfered with traditional customs, and created distinct problems for women.

As early as 1850, the colonial authorities in British North America began to keep lists to identify individual Aboriginal people and the bands to which they belonged. After Confederation, this list became what is now known as the Indian Register. To this day a senior civil servant, the Registrar, administers this exhaustive list at the head office of the recently renamed Department of Aboriginal Affairs and Northern Development, formerly the Department of Indian Affairs. Computer files have replaced nineteenth-century ledger books, but the content is the same. The Indian Register contains the names of all status Indians in the country: dates of birth, death, marriage and divorce, as well as records related to people who move from one band to another. If your name is not on the Indian Register, the federal government will not recognize your claim to the benefits of "Indian status" or "treaty status." Only "registered Indians" can claim rights,[4] and the government has the last say over who is included in this register.

Canada has made twenty major changes to the *Indian Act* over the past 136 years. Frequently these amendments involved a new definition of who could be a registered Indian. In the first version of the

Indian Act in 1876, the definition of Indian emphasized male lineage even though many tribal groups followed matrilineal lineage and recognized the authority of women in clans. The government rule defined an Indian as any male person of Indian blood reputed to belong to a band, any child of such a person and any woman lawfully married to such a person. At first if an Indian woman married a non-Indian, she lost her registered status but she did not necessarily lose her rights in practice. That hard day would come.

Canada continued to whittle away the membership rights of registered Indians in its first century. In 1894, for example, the government amended the Act to remove band control of non-Aboriginal people living on the reserve. In 1920, the government gave itself permission to remove the treaty rights of any status Indian deemed fit for involuntary "enfranchisement." A man or woman could be removed from the register, and denied the right to live on a reserve, while their descendants could lose all claim to treaty status—at the whim of a local Indian Agent, a white civil servant with considerable authority. Even if individuals wanted to challenge an unfair decision in a Canadian court, they were denied a fair opportunity. *Indian Act* amendments in 1927 made it an offence to solicit funds for Indian legal claims without a special licence from the Superintendent-General of Indian Affairs. Effectively, this meant an end to lawsuits to correct injustices.

Through its first century, the *Indian Act* and its regulations restricted every aspect of life for individuals, from birth to death, with a series of Thou Shalt Nots. For a time in the nineteenth century First Nations citizens could not travel between reserves, or from their reserve into a nearby city or town, without a pass from the local Indian Agent. On the prairies, First Nations farmers could not sell their farm produce without an Indian Agent's permission. The government did not allow First Nations citizens to practise their spiritual ceremonies; certain traditional dances and potlatches were outlawed. Treaty Indians were not allowed to drink alcohol or enter bars. After an *Indian Act* amendment in 1930 they were not even allowed to enter a pool hall too frequently. They could not obtain credit or a bank loan to begin a business as they could not offer collectively-owned land or housing as collateral. They could fight for Canada in two World Wars, and die for their country, but they could not collect the veterans' benefits that other Canadian soldiers took for granted. Until 1960, registered Indians could only vote in federal elections if they gave up their treaty rights; they could not vote in a provincial election in Alberta until 1967. Under all of these oppressive regulations, many frustrated treaty members voluntarily surrendered their treaty status during this era to obtain equal rights with other Canadians. This meant that their children and all of their unborn descendants lost treaty rights that the families valued highly, especially the right to live on a reserve.

If these rules were harsh, the *Indian Act*'s discrimination against women contained even more arbitrary punishment. Before 1950, the Government of Canada had invented narrow categories to sort out Aboriginal people for administrative purposes. The Department of Indian Affairs used the term "white-ticket holder" to refer to an individual with registered Indian status. A "blue-ticket holder" was the government term to describe Métis persons or non-registered Indians, many of whom lived on reserves. A "red-ticket holder" was the government's label for a woman with registered Indian status who married a man without Indian status.

The worst setback for women came in 1951. Parliament amended the *Indian Act* again to establish a more official government register of all Indian people, and redefined those who would be eligible to be described as "status" or "registered Indians." From that day on, only band members registered under the *Indian Act* had the legal right to live on-reserve, to share in band resources, own or inherit property, vote for band council and chief, or be buried on the reserve. These rules would be strictly enforced. In the *Indian Act* amendments, the federal government denied all red-ticket holders and their children the rights that came with Indian status.

And then came the raw sexual discrimination of Section 12(1)(b).

What did the section say? It was a handful of devastating words, a legislative sting that cheated thousands of First Nations women and their descendants of their birthright. In essence, the rule said that any First Nations woman who married a non-status Indian, a Métis man or a non-Aboriginal man would lose her legal Indian status immediately after her marriage, regardless of her ancestry. That meant she could not live on the reserve where she was born, she could not inherit her parents' house, or any property in her home community. She was forbidden to speak up about a local issue at a band meeting, or vote for a new chief and council. She could not claim her fair share of the band's money and natural resources for herself or her children. From the day she lost her registered status, she and her family would have no access to education or health benefits recognized under Canada's treaties with the First Nations. She could not be buried on her home reserve when she died, and her descendants had no claim to treaty rights or registered Indian status anywhere in the country. The "double mother" clause also stipulated that a person whose parents married on or after September 4, 1951 and whose mother and paternal grandmother had not been registered Indians before their marriages, would lose status and band membership on his or her twenty-first birthday.

In practice, this arbitrary change in the law meant forced exile from a home community, and a harsher and more difficult life.

In contrast, under the same section of the *Indian Act*, any registered Indian man could marry a woman with no Aboriginal ancestry at all—a war bride from England or Holland, say, or a young Ukrainian immigrant from the next town—and his wife would gain all of his treaty rights for herself, her children and future generations of her family. After his death, his non-Aboriginal widow could still claim treaty rights and the right to live on a reserve.

"The plain truth? The law just wasn't fair," Kathleen said. Yet the Canadian government defended this rigid discrimination against First Nations women for more than thirty years, through numerous court cases, and despite an appeal to the United Nations Human

Rights Committee.[5] The federal government capitulated only two months before the sexual equality provisions of Canada's new *Charter of Rights and Freedoms* came into force in 1985.

As young women who came of age in the 1950s, Nellie and Kathleen found themselves caught in the worst period of this *Indian Act* discrimination. Born into influential Cree families in Saddle Lake, each woman lost her Indian status after marriage. They married men who had just as much First Nations ancestry as they did, but whose families had lost treaty status over the years for various reasons related to the definitions in the *Indian Act*. In their frustration, Nellie and Kathleen found many allies—including Jenny Shirt Margetts, who like them had also been born on the Saddle Lake reserve in Alberta, and Mary Two-Axe Earley, a Mohawk activist who had been born on the Kahnawake reserve in Quebec. They, too, had been stripped of treaty status after marriage, and they were just as angry about it.

A vigorous Aboriginal rights movement, intertwined with a cultural renaissance, sprang up across Canada in the 1960s and 1970s. Its young leaders led protest marches and sit-ins, wrote stinging rebukes to government policy, researched new land claims, created new media of their own, and revitalized Aboriginal organizations to confront Ottawa about a century of broken promises. Many of these young people had developed a collective sense of injustice in residential school, not to mention sturdy survival skills, a network of contacts, and a streak of rebellion. Their generation began a determined search for justice, creating a new political movement to reclaim Aboriginal rights and treaty rights, to fight the chronic poverty on reserves and to claim a fair share of the nation's land and resources. Their efforts coincided with other international civil rights movements of the same era, especially the parallel efforts of Native Americans and African Americans to overcome similar racial discrimination in the United States. Across borders, the activists inspired one another.

Discontent rose to a boiling point in 1969. The Liberal government of Prime Minister Pierre Trudeau introduced a policy document known as the White Paper on *Indian Act* reform. It proposed the abolition of the *Indian Act*, the rejection of unsettled land claims and the termination of treaty and Aboriginal rights from the First Nations citizens who would henceforth be considered as another ethnic group in Canada. Harold Cardinal, the twenty-four-year-old Cree leader of the Indian Association of Alberta, led a delegation of chiefs to Ottawa to oppose the idea. He outlined their strenuous opposition in a document called *Citizens Plus*, later nicknamed the Red Paper (1970), and he wrote *The Unjust Society*, a book that quickly became a Canadian bestseller. As public pressure grew across the country, the government backed down and withdrew the proposal.

Disinherited First Nations women began to reach out to one another in this atmosphere of rising activism. Kathleen remembers hearing from a friend in the late 1960s about a brave woman named Jeannette Corbière Lavell who was challenging Section 12(1)(b) in Ontario. From her home in Edmonton, Kathleen wrote letters to women who might answer her questions about this campaign. Nellie encountered her old friend from Saddle Lake, Jenny Margetts, and together the Edmonton women began to contact other women across Alberta who had lost their treaty rights. At first they had no money to spend on an organization, lawsuits or lobbying campaigns, but they had enough courage and willpower to challenge an oppressive law. They gathered in each other's homes, often with their young children playing in the same room, to discuss the problem and to write letters of protest together. They met some young, idealistic law students, Jim Robb and Jean McBean, who were willing to help them, and they raised funds for a determined lobbying campaign. Later they organized a series of national conferences, and met Mary Two-Axe Earley, the trailblazer from Kahnawake who had founded Equal Rights for Indian Women as a provincial organization in Quebec in 1967.

Together, they organized Indian Rights for Indian Women in Alberta as a national organization in 1971, opened an office in the corner of a west-end welding business in Edmonton, and travelled to Ottawa many times to press their case with anyone who would listen.

Against considerable odds, they built informal alliances and a national organization that stretched like a lifeline from Caroline Wesley on Haida Gwaii off the west coast of British Columbia to Philomena Aulotte, Philomena Deschamps Ross and Agnes Gendron in Alberta; to Yvonne Bédard, Jeannette Corbière Lavell and Monica Turner in Ontario; to Mary Two-Axe Earley in Quebec, to Sandra Lovelace and the Maliseet activists on the Tobique reserve in New Brunswick. Soon other women joined the movement in small towns and cities from coast to coast. Together they fought that loathed section of the *Indian Act* until they got rid of it.

The most painful part of their fight? Aside from the federal government, they had to challenge opponents within their own First Nations, often men and women in their own families, who had no sympathy for their position. They also had to take on the male power structure of the National Indian Brotherhood, the organization that preceded the Assembly of First Nations, as well as the male-dominated treaty organizations in most provinces.

Why did these male leaders oppose them? Perhaps only they can answer that question. In her testimony to the Royal Commission on Aboriginal Peoples in 1992, Nellie concluded that many First Nations people of her generation had been "thoroughly brainwashed" to accept the *Indian Act*'s imposition on their lives. In some way they had swallowed a colonial mentality in residential school, she said later, and they didn't seem to realize it. "This was not really the fault of the leadership, but the fault of the Canadian government." Male leaders seemed convinced they were defending treaty rights when they opposed the women who wanted those rights back.

This was also a combative era when Canadian feminists were challenging all kinds of restrictions on women, and gender inequality in their society. Many men in positions of authority adopted a stubborn, defensive position in response—and Aboriginal male leaders were no different. Some maintained the sexist notion that women who had made their own beds in marriages with outsiders should have to lie in them. Kathleen wonders whether the National Indian Brotherhood, which had just started to make headway in negotiations with the federal government in the early 1970s, distrusted a group of urban women who communicated a strong and yet entirely different message to Ottawa. Nellie adds: "I think it was fear that we would spread our influence to their communities if we were reinstated. That's absolutely the truth. I always thought that's what it was. Fear."

When questioned by news reporters, male and female opponents of Indian Rights for Indian Women would point to overcrowded reserves with poor housing where far too many families lived in poverty. What would happen in their communities, they asked, if the government reinstated thousands of women and their children? They said they feared an influx of non-status relatives would put an impossible strain on First Nations' limited financial resources.

The women in the Indian Rights for Indian Women movement did not put one another in the government's rigid status categories. While Nellie and Kathleen were naturally indignant about an assault on treaty rights, they recognized that First Nations women suffered the same *Indian Act* discrimination in areas of Canada where no treaties had ever been signed, specifically British Columbia, the Yukon, and large regions of the Northwest Territories. The women formed a new network that crossed tribal lines and provincial boundaries.

Canada and its history books make a firm distinction between the First Nations, the indigenous tribal peoples of the territory that became Canada, and the Métis, a distinct Aboriginal people that emerged in western North America from the unions of First Nations women and European men after the 1600s. The activists understood that the classification of families was not always so clear-cut. Nellie and Kathleen point out that many families identified long ago by the government as "non-status Indians" or "Métis" had actually been cheated of their treaty birthright by the random decisions of a federal Indian Agent in their community, that local bureaucrat who could strike a family name off a Band List with unchecked authority. For example, the *Indian Act* permitted these government agents to "protest" the treaty status of "illegitimate" children of reserve women with treaty rights, and remove the children from band membership.

Sometimes the descendants of these disinherited First Nations families never knew about the lost treaty rights, and grew up in cities and towns assuming they were Métis. This was also true of children with treaty rights who were taken away from their families on reserves and placed into orphanages and residential schools, as well as the Aboriginal children later lost to the provincial child welfare systems and white adoptive homes in the infamous "scoop" of the 1960s and 1970s. Several generations were removed and isolated from their traditional way of learning the oral history of their community. Thousands of Aboriginal children grew up with no firm idea of their family lineage, their clan or kinship, their community of origin, their tribal affiliation, or even their own name at birth. This was the theft that Indian Rights for Indian Women wanted to fight most strenuously—the theft of a child's true Aboriginal identity.

The activists of Indian Rights for Indian Women encountered many disappointments in their long fight for justice. Jeannette Corbière Lavell, a young woman born into the Wikwemikong band of Anishinabek people on Manitoulin Island, and Yvonne Bédard, born a member of the Six Nations, fought separate cases against Section 12(1)(b) through the courts. The Supreme Court of Canada ruled against them in a narrow decision in 1973, finding that the *Canadian Bill of Rights*[6] did not supersede the *Indian Act*. Sandra Lovelace, a Wolastoqiyik or Maliseet from the Tobique Nation in New Brunswick, filed a complaint against Canada in 1977 with the United Nations Human Rights Committee in Geneva, Switzerland. The tribunal subsequently found Canada in breach of Article 27 of the *International Covenant on Civil and Political Rights*.[7] And yet still the federal government would not budge.

In another disheartening moment, Mary Two-Axe Earley—by
now a nationally recognized opponent of the gender discrimination
in the *Indian Act*—received an eviction notice from her home on the
Kahnawake reserve in 1975. While all of these women appealed for
support through the media to the Canadian public, they felt they had
made little progress by the end of the decade. Still they kept trying.

Finally a pent-up longing for change collided with an historic
opportunity.

The first Quebec referendum on sovereignty-association in May
1980 pushed the federal government and nine other provinces into
a fevered attempt to renew Canadian federalism in order to keep the
country together. Time almost stopped in this country for two years
as Canadians argued fiercely about a plan to redraft the Constitution.
The country had failed repeatedly in previous attempts to breathe
new life into that dusty old *British North America Act, 1867*. This time
there seemed to be a pressing deadline. While the prime minister
and premiers argued for months over a new division of powers and
an amending formula, and the provinces mounted court challenges,
the Canadian public began an unprecedented debate about the
protection of human rights in every form. Women mounted a determined campaign to have a guarantee of sexual equality entrenched in
the new *Charter of Rights and Freedoms*. The First Nations, Métis and
Inuit seized this rare moment in history to push hard for entrenched
recognition of Aboriginal and treaty rights.

Pointing to the law of the land that they detested, the Indian
Rights for Indian Women movement could argue that Aboriginal
women had endured more gender discrimination, and a greater theft
of Aboriginal and Treaty rights, than any other people in the country.
Suddenly they had the floor. The Sandra Lovelace case was fresh in
the public mind. Mary Two-Axe Earley, Jenny Margetts and Nellie
Carlson returned to Ottawa to push their case. People began to listen.

Few Canadians of this era had received any instruction at all in
school about Aboriginal history or Aboriginal rights. Now every time
they turned on the television set, they heard complex debates among

Aboriginal leaders about the best way to protect historic rights. This sudden immersion course was long overdue. Perhaps it was the first time that the entire country recognized the cultural and political diversity, and the differences of opinion, alive and thriving within the indigenous communities of Canada. Chiefs from Alberta and Saskatchewan went to England to lobby the British Parliament and to appeal to the courts to block patriation of the Constitution before the Crown settled its debts to the First Nations on neglected treaties. Métis leaders from the prairies worked just as hard to see their long-ignored Aboriginal rights recognized and guaranteed in the *Charter*; patriation couldn't happen soon enough for them.

After eighteen months of intense discussion and lobbying, involving just about everyone, Canada settled on a fresh set of compromises. The new *Constitution Act* was proclaimed on Parliament Hill on April 17, 1982. The new *Charter of Rights and Freedoms* became the country's primary law, entrenched in the Constitution. It guaranteed women's equality rights, as well as existing treaty and Aboriginal rights, so the *Indian Act* discrimination against women could no longer be permitted or justified. The federal government had no choice but to bend. The Indian Rights for Indian Women activists could taste sweet victory at last.

Unfortunately, Section 15 on equality rights did not come into force for three years, which allowed more time for delay. The Liberal government's first attempt to eliminate the discrimination in the *Indian Act*, Bill c-47, died on a single vote in the Senate cast by an Inuit Senator Charlie Watt in 1984. This brought crushing frustration to the women. They were exasperated. The government tried again the following year, and finally succeeded to the great pride and delight of the activists who had fought the repressive, old rule for so long.

Bill c-31[8] was a compromise. "It wasn't perfect," said Nellie, "but it was a start." The new amendments removed overt sexual discrimination from the *Indian Act*, restored Indian status and membership rights to disinherited Aboriginal people, and increased First Nations local authority. However, the federal government maintained control over who would be registered as an Indian, and the rights that would flow from membership.

Women who lost Indian status through marriage, and their children, could apply for reinstatement to a General List, and a Band List. The reforms also allowed Aboriginal people whose families had lost status for various other reasons to apply for limited status based on their ancestry and lineage. The government said that the First Nations could determine their own membership rules, and regulate who could live on the reserve. Many urban women who reclaimed Indian status, including Nellie and Kathleen, had no interest in moving back to a reserve. Even so, the change in the law provoked a new round of resistance from some chiefs and councils who altered membership codes in an attempt to keep them out.

Immediately controversial, Bill C-31 brought a severe reaction from three oil-rich First Nations in Alberta that distributed lucrative energy royalties to their members. The Sawridge, Ermineskin and Tsuu T'ina First Nations launched legal action against the Government of Canada to challenge the rights of band members reinstated under Bill C-31. When the federal courts ruled against them after an eight-month hearing, Sawridge Chief Walter Twinn described the ruling as "the most anti-Indian pronouncement of recent judicial history" and promised to appeal the decision.[9] For her part, Kathleen Steinhauer launched her own lawsuit in the Federal Court of Canada to be reinstated on the Band List of the Saddle Lake Cree Nation, a case she finally won in 1999.

In their stories, Nellie and Kathleen see positive and negative consequences of Bill C-31. They are delighted that an estimated 162,000 disinherited individuals are back in the fold of the First Nations, and are able to exercise their treaty and Aboriginal rights. They are happy that these people can benefit from the practical side of status recognition: increased health and education assistance in particular. They say the best part of the change is that more families can pass on these rights to future generations of children.

They do regret that some First Nations still invent restrictive membership codes and pursue court cases to keep families from living on reserves, and that urban families often find it difficult to claim their treaty rights off the reserve. They don't like the way people who have reclaimed their status after 1985 are nicknamed "Bill c-31 Indians"—which they see as yet another label that isolates and splits First Nations people into rigid identity categories determined by the government. They detested a new restriction, the so-called "second generation cut-off,"[10] in a more recent amendment of the *Indian Act*, which they believed would rob future generations of their rights. Watching the newspapers and television news broadcasts, they admire the hard work of a new generation of activists— especially Sharon McIvor's campaign for the disinherited people still excluded from full status.[11] In their final conversations with me before Kathleen's death, the two elders emphasized that the discrimination continues, and must be challenged.

Nellie Carlson and Kathleen Steinhauer nurtured four hopes for this book.

First they wanted to honour their extraordinary friend Jenny Margetts, who led and inspired Indian Rights for Indian Women in western Canada through many challenges, and who died in 1991. They believe Jenny's contributions—like those of other First Nations women in Canada—have not received the public recognition they deserve.

Secondly, they wanted to put their own version of events on the public record. They are disturbed at the number of people who take credit for getting rid of the *Indian Act*'s discriminatory clause, when some of these people did nothing to assist them, or actively opposed them during the turbulent 1970s. They have included an Honour Roll at the end of this book to name the many forgotten women they contend did the hard work through two decades of determined political lobbying, failed court cases, harassment and disappointments. They also want to pay tribute to their lawyers and other fine Canadians who supported their struggle with practical assistance behind the scenes.

Third, they hoped the stories in this book would remind young First Nations, Métis and Inuit citizens across Canada of their enduring obligation to protect treaty and Aboriginal rights. They speak of treaty rights first, but they also ask the next generation to protect the integrity of Aboriginal land, languages, cultures and spiritual traditions. They say it is not up to the Canadian government to legislate an individual's identity, or to divide families through the narrow definitions of Canada's *Indian Act*, the Bill c-31 amendments of 1985, or the Bill c-3 amendments of 2010. In dozens of different ways, throughout this book, Kathleen and Nellie return to this same strong message to Aboriginal young people: You, alone, have the right to define who you are.

"We had to go to court many times," Kathleen said. "Our learning experience might be a guide to those in court, or those who feel the challenge that the law is against the voice of women."

Finally, the two elders make one more request of the next generation. They would like university professors and their students to investigate Canada's historic discrimination against Aboriginal women, and to produce new and comprehensive academic research and analysis for the public. So many important questions remain unanswered.

◆ It is a cold winter day in Edmonton. Imagine that you are sipping hot soup, and listening to Kathleen Steinhauer and Nellie Carlson as they begin to tell an important story. A blizzard will keep you here all afternoon while time stops. Would you like some bannock? It's hot from the stove, and ready to dip into your soup. Nellie is pounding her fist on the table, and laughing hard, as she describes the day she shocked former Prime Minister Pierre Trudeau at a private meeting in Ottawa. "Mary Two-Axe kicked me in the shins under the table for saying what I said to him, and I could hardly walk out of there!" she says. Kathleen has heard this story before. "Oh, *nôtokwêw*, you embarrass me sometimes," she says, laughing too. Kathleen uses the Cree word for "old lady" with affection because this is her favourite nickname for her cousin. In the same way, Nellie calls her Kay. They begin to tell their story about the Cree treaty rights that were taken from them, and reclaimed, through a lifetime's struggle that is not over yet.

It is a privilege to listen to them, to sit beside them, to learn from them.

LINDA GOYETTE
Spring, 2012

kîkinâw / our home

1

 **Daughters of Saddle Lake**

BORN INTO THE SADDLE LAKE CREE NATION in the Treaty Six
territory of western Canada,[1] Nellie Carlson and Kathleen Steinhauer
have lived with their families in Edmonton for more than forty
years, but they retain a strong bond with their birthplace and home
community, located about 200 kilometres northeast of the city.

Nellie is the granddaughter of the late Thomas Makokis, a Saddle
Lake traditional chief in the 1920s, and the daughter of the late Frank
Makokis and Marjorie Jackson Makokis, who asked Nellie on her
deathbed to defend the rights of children. Nellie's great-grandmother
was a wife of Onchaminahos, Chief Little Hunter, who signed Treaty
Six at Fort Pitt on September 9, 1876 on behalf of his Cree band.
She is particularly proud of the chief's words at the signing cere-
mony, which were recorded and translated from Cree as follows: "I
am thankful for the children for they will prosper. All the children
who are sitting here hope that the Great Spirit will look down upon
us as one."

Kathleen traces her First Nations ancestry to an early Cree couple of the fur trade who lived on the prairies before the signing of Treaty Six. Her great-grandmother, Angeline Rose, born around 1851, belonged to the Papaschase Cree Nation near Fort Edmonton. Angeline married Peter Apow, born around 1844, and the couple lived for most of their lives at Whitefish Lake and nearby Saddle Lake.

Kathleen's father, Ralph Steinhauer,[2] was born at Morley on the Stoney Nakoda reserve in southern Alberta. He would grow up to become the chief of the Saddle Lake Cree for many years, and eventually the first Lieutenant-Governor of Alberta of First Nations descent. When Ralph was five years old, his father Josiah Apow died. His mother subsequently married James Steinhauer who adopted her children, and gave them his surname.

As a result of her father's adoption, Kathleen belongs to the large Steinhauer family with deep roots in Saddle Lake and Whitefish Lake. The Cree family has a German surname for interesting reasons. Their famous ancestor, Henry Bird Steinhauer, was born Sowengisik in the Anishinabek Nation in northern Ontario in 1811, but he changed his surname to Steinhauer in 1828 to please an American benefactor who had offered to pay for his education. The young Steinhauer moved west to Norway House, Manitoba as a Methodist missionary and married a Cree woman, Seeseb Mamanuwartum, whose English name was Jessie Joyful. Moving west again, the couple established the Whitefish Lake Mission near Saddle Lake in 1858, and raised twelve children. Jessie died at the age of ninety-two in 1910.

Nellie and Kathleen are cousins through the Apow family. They have kinship ties through their birth families, and through marriage, to members of many other First Nations, including the Papaschase, Enoch, Michel and Onion Lake First Nations in central Alberta and Saskatchewan; to the Kainai and Tsuu T'ina tribes in the Treaty Seven territory of southern Alberta; and to many Métis families. Through her maternal line, Kathleen is also descended from early prairie settlers. Her mother, Isabel Davidson Steinhauer, and her

First Nations chiefs with two western missionaries pose for portrait during their visit to Toronto in 1886. Left to right: Rev. John McDougall; Samson, Cree Chief; Pakan, known also as James Seenum, one of the founders of Saddle Lake Cree Nation; Rev. Henry Bird Steinhauer; Jonas Goodstoney, Stoney chief. Author Nellie Carlson has kinship ties with Pakan. Author Kathleen Steinhauer's father, born Ralph Apow, was adopted into the Steinhauer family. [Glenbow Archives, NA–4216–33]

paternal grandmother, Amelia Mumford Apow, were American-born women of Scottish descent who married Cree men with treaty rights; consequently they became treaty Indians according to Canadian law.

Kathleen and Nellie have known one another since they were children. To learn more about their interconnected lineage, see the family tree chart at the back of this book.

◆ Nellie Carlson

I was born Nellie Makokis on July 3, 1927, on a Treaty Day[3] on the Saddle Lake reserve. My father went and got my treaty money, and I got my first five dollar on the day of my birth. For that very reason, I have strongly defended my treaty rights all my life.

We were taught to respect the elders, and not to question them. At the age of two or three, I discovered my echo. I grew up in a loving, affectionate, gentle home. If there was discipline needed, you were talked to in a firm way. I had siblings, my sister Ruth, and four who passed away. Three boys and a girl died. They were older.

In 1924, my grandpa, Thomas Makokis, was the traditional chief at Saddle Lake. The government worked on him for two years. The United Church minister and the priest worked on him day and night to give up [agree to a reserve land surrender] and sign a document. Finally my Grandpa signed the document to sell some land, to accommodate people from Ireland who had the help of the *Soldier Settlement Act*.[4]

Uncle Ralph [Steinhauer] used to tease me when I was very small. When he saw me, he used to sing "Darling Nellie Gray" even on Treaty Days. I would hide behind a wagon when I saw him coming.

One of my earliest memories was in the early 1930s. I was taken by my family to a traditional Round Dance, held away from the reserve, away from the Indian Agent. Around 1930, the Indian Agents told people at Saddle Lake there was a new law. There would be no more large gatherings, no sweat lodges or Sun Dances, no potlatch allowed for the bands on the coast, no long houses down

People from Saddle Lake crossing the North Saskatchewan River on the Shandro Ferry. Date unknown.

Top left: The wedding of Jean-Marie Cardinal and Anna Houle with the groom's brother, Elmer Carlson, as best man and Sophie Woods as bridesmaid. Bottom left: A family at Saddle Lake.

Below: Ceremonial dance at Saddle Lake reserve in 1933. While the Government of Canada outlawed First Nations traditional ceremonies, sweat lodges, potlatches and dances during this period, the Cree of Saddle Lake preserved their spiritual practices in private, away from the eyes of the local Indian Agent. [Glenbow Archives, NA–783–2]

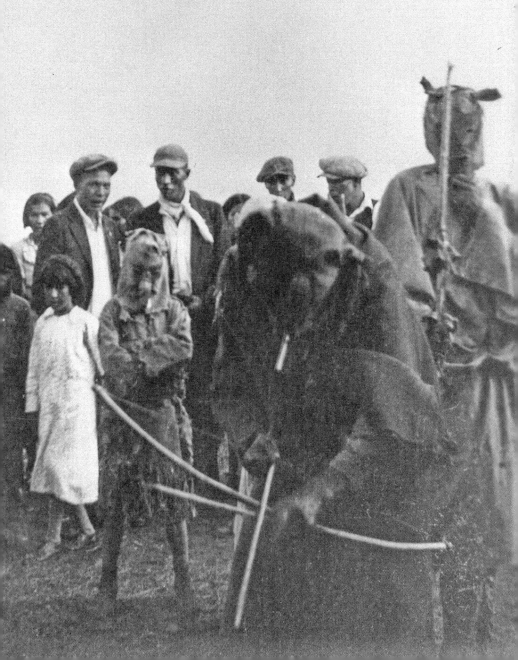

Thomas Makokis and Anna Hunter Makokis, grandparents of Nellie Carlson. Thomas served for a time as the chief of Saddle Lake Cree Nation.

east.[5] I loved this [the gatherings] when I was small. I asked to go. I begged to see the drummers; I wanted to dance. I remember Baptiste Cardinal and Johnny Brittain. We had to give money if we wanted to go, to give blankets to visitors. On the reserve, Treaty Days were always in July. People at Saddle Lake would pitch tents, and there would be a sports day, horse racing, dances. We would have open-air Round Dances by the fire, and the men took turns singing. Visitors would come from other reserves. The RCMP came to give out the treaty money, and sometimes something for the kids. The five dollar treaty money, the parents kept. We got a little to spend, just coins, on ice cream or a treat. The two RCMP officers would come in their red serge to give the treaty money out.

What I know about my history is what my mother told me. My mother said my grandfather was Thomas Makokis. His wife was Anna Hunter. They had only one child and that was my father, Frank. It is my Cree upbringing, and the knowledge of it, that helps me in my life.

◆ Kathleen Steinhauer

My name is Kathleen Amelia Jean Steinhauer. I was born on May 6, 1932, the third child of Ralph and Isabel Steinhauer, at Saddle Lake reserve.

My father Ralph Steinhauer was a Saddle Lake Cree band member. My mother was Isabel Davidson, an American of Scottish descent who came out to Alberta because she had bad lungs. She worked in a bank in Provost for two or three years, then she went to the Camrose Normal School to take teacher training for a year, and then she moved to Vilna to teach. My father worked in the nearby General Store that included the Post Office. He had some difficulty being sworn in as a postal clerk because he was considered a ward of the Canadian government as a treaty Indian. They just wouldn't hire treaty Indians. My uncles couldn't work at the telegraph office and had the same problem. In 1925, my father hired a lawyer in Toronto to try to make it possible, and they finally reversed that decision.

My father saw my mother when he brought her the mail, and of course it was such a small town. They couldn't help knowing each other. They got married, and she became a Saddle Lake band member. I was the third girl in the family. My older sister Muriel was born in 1929, and my sister Doreen followed in 1931 and June was born in 1937. We were born as members of the Saddle Lake Cree, and we were all band members with treaty rights until we married. My father was named chief in the year of my birth.

In 1945, my parents adopted a little boy who was born to a woman whose husband was off to war. My mother said they went to see him and he melted their hearts, and they brought him home. They

Below: The Steinhauer girls and their mother. Left to right: Muriel, June, Doreen, Kathleen and their mother Isabel Steinhauer.

Top right: Francis Jackson and Katherine Shirt at their wedding with family and friends. Bottom right: Ralph Shirt and Edna Carlson at their wedding with Peter Shirt and Mary Steinhauer. The groom was a stepbrother of Nellie Carlson and the bride was the sister of Elmer Carlson.

Left to right: Kathleen, Muriel and Doreen Steinhauer.

named him Kenneth Davidson Steinhauer. Nellie was actually there when he was born. She helped with the birth and cared for him....I have known Nellie for as long as I can remember.

I guess I was an outgoing, curious little girl, always asking questions. My first memory must have come when I was two or three. It was after the harvest. My grandmother bought a piano, and sent it to my mother. It was stored at the river because there was no bridge at the time, and you had to ford the river. Once the bridge was built, they brought the piano over by lumber wagon. I remember standing there and watching, so excited. My parents were later quite surprised that I remembered this because I was two-and-a-half years old, or three at the most. My uncles, my Dad and Laurie, my grandfather's cousin, arrived with the piano, and brought it into the house. Laurie had muscles like Popeye. I was told to sit on the fence to watch the building of a new room to accommodate the piano.

We lived in a two-room house. There always seemed to be family there, always aunts and uncles. They would read the comics to us. It was a quiet atmosphere. I don't remember anybody shouting at us to discipline us. There was a way then: there was a gentle ridicule to remind you that a certain behaviour just wasn't done.

We had the only piano in the area. My mother had voice training in a choir, and played the piano, so when the children of the district were practicing for Christmas concerts or had competitive festivals, the school would send them to my mother for music lessons. And yet the school board wouldn't let us go to that district school because we were treaty Indians. Actually, my older sister Muriel went to the school for two years and then she was expelled. She was taught by a Métis woman, Miss Brosseau, whose grandmother was a L'Hirondelle. Miss Brosseau kept her in school for a time, but when the school found out, she wasn't allowed to continue. I always kidded my sister about being expelled at the age of eight.

My parents talked about what to do. "Where will we send them? Foisy? St. Laurent? Lafond?" No school would have us. It was feared my father had TB at that time. He was sick in 1937, confined to a tent for isolation. My sister June was an infant of only a few months. My parents decided that the only place we could go to school was to the residential school in Edmonton.

Surviving Residential School

IT IS HARD TO ACCEPT that this country once betrayed its children, and ignored their suffering. By the time little Nellie Makokis and Kathleen Steinhauer walked through the huge front door of Edmonton Indian Residential School in the early 1930s, thousands of Aboriginal children were living in more than eighty boarding schools across the nation. They had no say, no voice, and no choice. The government had passed a law in 1920 to make attendance mandatory. If families kept their children out of the residential schools, the police, clergy or a government Indian Agent would arrive to take them back.

Canada invented the Indian residential school system to force First Nations, Métis and Inuit children to abandon their languages and traditional culture, and to assimilate into the wider society. Funded by the federal government, and run by Canada's churches, these boarding schools proved to be an enduring curse on thousands of children, their families and their communities through subsequent generations. In 1857, the *Act to Encourage the Gradual*

Civilization of Indian Tribes in this Province, and to Amend the Laws Relating to Indians (commonly called the *Gradual Civilization Act*) set up the framework for the schools.[1] The consequences of this system are suffered to this day.

As children, Nellie and Kathleen were in slightly different situations. By law, Nellie had to go to the school for a decade, and emerged as a young adult. Kathleen and her two sisters were able to withdraw from the school after three years, possibly because they lived on a farm bordering the reserve, and also because their mother, Isabel Steinhauer, was non-Aboriginal and had challenged the principal angrily about the poor quality of care at the school. The Steinhauers eventually withdrew their children from residential school, and taught them at home for two years. Later, the Steinhauer girls were able to enrol at Duclos Mission School near Bonnyville, Alberta and proceeded to high school at Alberta College in Edmonton. As a boarding student in the city, Kathleen completed her Grade Twelve at Victoria High School, a public education that her out-of-town parents had to pay to obtain. She never forgot her beginnings at the residential school.

Catholic children at Saddle Lake usually attended Blue Quill's Indian Residential School just beyond the reserve's western boundary, but Protestant children like Nellie and Kathleen had to go to Edmonton Indian Residential School, located just north of the city in the neighbouring town of St. Albert. "Residential school was such a shock for us," remembers Kathleen. "All of us had the impression that the other ones—the kids in the other school—had it so much better. Better food, better clothing. But we didn't."

Both Nellie and Kathleen were physically abused at the school, and have carried its injuries—physical, emotional and cultural—throughout their lives. On June 11, 2008, the two women sat in front of their televisions in Edmonton, and listened to Prime Minister Stephen Harper offer the nation's formal apology in Parliament. "The treatment of children in Indian residential schools is a sad chapter in our history," he said. "Today, we recognize that this policy of assimilation was wrong, has caused great harm, and has no place in our country.

"The government now recognizes that the consequences of the Indian residential schools policy were profoundly negative and that this policy has had a lasting and damaging impact on Aboriginal culture, heritage and language," Harper said. "While some former students have spoken positively about their experiences at residential schools, these stories are far overshadowed by tragic accounts of the emotional, physical and sexual abuse and neglect of helpless children, and their separation from powerless families and communities."

Both Nellie and Kathleen wonder how many Canadians know what happened inside school buildings near their own homes, including the residential school they attended. The United Church of Canada ran the Edmonton Indian Residential School from 1925 to 1966. Eighty former students subsequently filed lawsuits against the federal government to address physical, emotional and severe sexual abuse they endured at the school. Many of the lawsuits accused Rev. James Clarence Ludford of sexual assault against boys. Ludford pleaded guilty to charges of gross indecency against a male student in 1960, was given a one-year suspended sentence and ordered to receive psychiatric care. The United Church fired him from the school, but subsequently employed him in another ministry in a First Nations community in Ontario. He died in 1990 before he could be charged in the other cases.

Substandard living conditions at Edmonton Indian Residential School were on record for decades, and little was done to improve them. In 1946—four years after Nellie left the school—Rev. E.J. Staley filed a report to his superiors after accepting a position as principal. He wrote: "Hundreds of panes of glass are broken. The plumbing is completely out of commission. Droppings from the toilet [are] coming through the roofs onto the main floor....There is not a decent mattress in the school. They are filthy and loathsome.

There is no clothing, not a pair of pants, not a shirt or shoe, not a suit of underwear nor any girls' clothing of any description."

Through the decades, similar reports reached authorities. A 1962 report from an Edmonton welfare services group complained of overcrowding, abusive staff and bad food. The Edmonton Indian Residential School did not close its doors until four years later. An unknown arsonist deliberately set fire to the old building in the summer of 2000, and it burned to the ground. Other former residential schools across Canada have burned down in similar arsons. Kathleen and Nellie believe they know why.

◆ Nellie Carlson

We had to grow up so fast. We had to go to the Edmonton Indian Residential School, after the age of five or six. I was sent there at the age of five years old. Hard, cold and violent was the way I was dealt with there. I didn't understand. There was no tenderness, not even a hug. As a small child, I spoke Cree at school and someone heard me. It was against the rules to speak Cree. This happened in 1933, when I was five. A staff member picked me up and put me on a table, then hit me hard, and I fell off the table and my back was seriously injured.

I was hit so hard I remember seeing stars. My back hurt so much after this happened.

I attended residential school from 1933 to 1942. In my school records it says, 1934 to 1943, but that is wrong. They did me a favour at residential school. I cannot see injustice now and do nothing. I have to act. That place did permanent injury to me: psychological damage and physical damage. But they did us all a favour—for some people like me, for many people, they strengthened our resolve. They were trying to domesticate us. Did it work? Hardly! None of us came out 100 per cent ready for university. It was a very poor education.

The big girls all had to work. They taught us how to make our beds, fold our nightgowns, things we had already learned at home. Some of the older girls got pregnant while they were at residential

Edmonton Indian Residential School, located in St. Albert on the northern outskirts of the city, housed thousands of Aboriginal children between 1925 and 1960.

school. This was hidden from their families. They bullied women into giving up their children.

◆ Kathleen Steinhauer

We were just terrified at first. I was so homesick. I was just sick with loneliness. It was raining. I was crying. And my Aunt May[2] found me. And she came and put me on her lap. I was hoping if I looked hard enough out the window I would see home. And she told me I was looking in the wrong direction. I was totally devastated.

Night after night, you'd hear the other children, crying themselves to sleep.

The white staff ate upstairs. The Indian staff ate downstairs. The food at the school was terrible. I remember Sundays at home and eating hot oatmeal with cream and brown sugar. At the school, they gave us cold, lumpy oatmeal with skim milk and a half-slice of old bread. I said something about it, and that was my mistake.

Girls at Edmonton Indian Residential School, date unknown. Both Nellie Carlson and Kathleen Steinhauer suffered harsh physical abuse in their years at a school they considered a prison.

Sarah Makokis was my little friend from Saddle Lake. Her mother was one of the Cardinals from the Wolf Lake Métis. One day I was sitting next to Sarah at the table in the dining room. They gave us this cold, lumpy oatmeal again. I put up my hand and said: "Could I have some brown sugar?" And the staff member hit me so hard I hit against the cement wall, and Sarah got hit too, and she was crying. The woman, she slapped me, and I fell backwards. Nobody was sitting on the other side so I went flying and hit the wall....This was my first horrible memory of that school.

I'd learned by then not to cry. That woman's favourite line was: "Stop crying or I'll hit you more." When we were punished, they put us in a space where they kept the mops, under the stairs. They would lock me in there. I would howl.

And I was not someone who sat in the corner and hid. I played with the other children. There was nobody around watching us at the time, and some of them couldn't speak English, so we spoke Cree....I was beaten by the supervisor and the matron for various things, and beaten for speaking Cree.

My grandmother lived in Edmonton, my mother's mother. I don't remember how many times she came to visit, but I do remember one day. I don't remember whether it was a church service upstairs, or a concert because sometimes the CGIT girls' group [Canadian Girls in Training] would come and perform a concert and distribute these oranges, one to each child. Anyway, I didn't know my grandmother was there. We were coming out of the hall, and we had to line up and walk out together. We weren't allowed to get out of line, or to talk. As I was a little girl, I went out first with the other small children. I noticed my grandmother sitting at the very back, right inside the door. The doors were open, and the Matron, the girls' supervisor, was standing right outside the door.

I whispered, "Grandmother!" The supervisor heard me, and just as soon as I got outside that door she whacked me across the head. I fell into the other child. I didn't dare cry out loud because it would only get worse. After that, you find out that there is no way out of this. This went on and on. I remember being totally overcome by the most devastating sense of despair. Just total despair and I was just a kid. Nobody should feel that way, especially not a little child. I just had no hope about anything.

I went in at the age of five and came out at the age of eight.

My sister, Doreen, got very, very ill in the school. She had pneumonia, and she almost died. My parents were never notified. I vaguely remember that I went to the infirmary with a scratch because I wanted to see her, and I peeked my head in there and got caught, and wham! Hit again.

I also remember in the middle of the night an awful lot of excitement. Doreen was still in the infirmary, and people were going up and down the hallway, and I heard voices up and down the stairs. What happened? They called the doctor in the middle of the night and they put her in an oxygen tent. There was a teacher there named Miss Spence, and she knew Grandmother quite well....Miss Spence happened to be there when Doreen was very sick, and she wrote to my mother and told her what she thought of the place, and what had happened to Doreen, and she said she was very concerned about us.

My mother had met Miss Spence and trusted her. When Mother came to get us she had a row with the principal. I was standing at the top of the stairs, just inside because I knew my mother was in the office, and I could hear this. My mother was a very reserved person but when she was angry you knew it. I was sure I had done something wrong. I could hear these voices, and I was terrified of the principal. My mother came out of that office and took us home.

We never had to go back. For the next two years my mother taught us with lessons from the Alberta Correspondence School Branch.

Residential school students at St. Albert, date unknown.

◆ The Residential School Experience

Kathleen and Nellie begin a conversation about residential school, and the government's financial compensation for former students.

NELLIE: I received a call on Friday. I am going to get $29,000. The
   lawyer will take 15 per cent. The reason I'm getting this is that
   I was knocked out when the teacher hit me. For nothing else.
   Myrtle Calahasen got $51,000 because she had to get an operation
   on her ears. They used to hit us around the ears when we spoke
   Cree. The federal government gave Maher Arar[3] $10.5 million for
   the terrible thing that Canada did to him. That's one person.

KATHLEEN: And Maher Arar is not going to lose the pain or suffering
   or the torture he suffered just because the Government of Canada
   paid him that money. We aren't either. When you're a child, and
   you're treated like that, you don't forget it. Nothing can take
   it away.

NELLIE: I asked for $1 million, $500,000 for the fact that I didn't
   get an education at that school, and $500,000 for what they did to

my back. Our children were the ones who paid the price for what happened to us. It's them that should be getting the benefit.

KATHLEEN: Yes, the descendants are in much worse shape than the people who went through it....We were permanently scarred after emotional, physical and psychological abuse, and this had a serious impact on our families and our communities.

NELLIE: Our days are numbered. If I have to go to hell for what I have said, I guess that's where I belong. If I go to hell, I want the people who did this to us to come with us.

KATHLEEN: When the churches talk about the word "healing," they forget how that word can sound to people who were abused in residential school. Who is going to want to go to the abusers for healing? No thank you!

NELLIE: And many people doing the counselling are not survivors of residential school themselves....In the school, you couldn't turn your back for a minute, for fear of the older kids and some teachers. There were some bullies. They reported us to Mrs. S. and they got their way with everything. A girl would come to you in the schoolyard and say, "How do you say such-and-such in Cree?" And you'd tell them. And they'd tell Mrs. S., "That girl was speaking Cree!" And you'd get hit.

KATHLEEN: You found out the rules by getting hit. Or by speaking Cree with other children. They'd say: "Hush, or you'll be hit!" There were runaways. The girls didn't run away as much. Some of the boys ran away.

NELLIE: Bobby Seenum and one girl ran away with another kid, Olive Olson, and a big girl with a growth on her neck. She took the road through Jasper and the police brought her back to school. We had to watch her being beaten so that we would get the message that this would happen to us if we ran away. We saw the growth on her neck bleeding.

KATHLEEN: One child was enuretic. She wet the bed nearly every night. She would get the strap every morning. That poor little girl. They would beat her through her wet nightie. [This beating dislocated the child's hip.] She limped. She never smiled after that.[4]

NELLIE: The runaways got severe beatings. Other children would die while they were at the school. We didn't know what happened to the bodies. Did they send their bodies home or did they bury them nearby for the economic savings of it?

KATHLEEN: You also have to think about the impact on the reserves. We lost our language. We lost the bonding with our parents. We'd get used to them in eight weeks in the summer, and then we had to go back.

There was a boy from Saddle Lake. I can see him yet. He wore a tweed cap, a jacket, pants. He worked for a farmer in the fall. He had saved his money and he thought he would go to Edmonton in the fall to work delivering milk by horse and wagon. In the city, he was leaning against the wall of the Alberta Hotel, just watching what was going on, and a policeman came along and said he would arrest him for vagrancy. It turned out he had to go to jail, a terrible punishment for doing nothing wrong. At Treaty time, we saw him in Saddle Lake again. We asked him, "What was it like in jail?" He said: "It wasn't that bad. It wasn't any worse than that school."

NELLIE: [Remembering another story from the school.] Old Mary chased the girls into the woods with a whip. They fell into the toilet holes.... I tell the lawyers, I grew up in a low-income home, but I was never hit. I never knew the feeling of it. I never saw an adult hitting a child in that [reserve] environment. Never did. But at that school...

KATHLEEN: The Catholic kids from our reserve—some of them— went to a convent in St. Albert. Some came to see us. They were pulling up their skirts, and showing us the pockets for their hand-kerchiefs. We wore dresses like sacks, made of denim. They looked like prison uniforms.

If those girls went to the bathroom the nuns would follow them. The girls couldn't speak because the nuns wouldn't let them speak to Protestant girls on their own.

The conversation shifts and Kathleen tells a story about First Nations and Métis children at the convent school in St. Albert. The Cunningham family is a prominent Métis family in Alberta.

KATHLEEN: In St. Albert, Walter Cunningham, Chester's[5] father, worked at the convent with the horses. They [the adults in charge of the school] went somewhere with a team of horses and a wagon. They took some kids along. The white kids could ride in the wagon and the Indian kids had to walk behind. The white driver had to go back for some reason. Walter Cunningham put all the Indian kids on the wagon, and he made the white kids walk behind. They were mad!

Kathleen then speaks of other students, Emma Memnook, later Emma Minde of Hobbema,[6] and Harriet Wood. Some conversation takes place in Cree before the two women return to speaking in English.

KATHLEEN: When they came to Edmonton, they quietly asked each other if they spoke Cree....Children would be okay in the morning, but by nightfall they would be dying to speak in their own language. Some of the students just shut their minds. They wouldn't speak their language for fear of punishment.

NELLIE: When the staff wasn't around, we spoke Cree in the playroom and playground. Worst of all, I used to hear very good stories and legends at home, but not at school. Do you think I know anything now? I don't. That's what we lost.

KATHLEEN: I understand Cree better than I can say it. A lot of it was just being away from home for so long.

NELLIE: Myrtle [Calahasen] was just four when she went to residential school. Sarah R. was four. They were little. They lost more. If residential school teaches you anything, it teaches you how to endure. It wrecks your personality. It makes you determined to get the best of them. You are so determined to survive.

3

 Love, Matrimony, and
the *Indian Act*

27

YOUNG NELLIE MAKOKIS AND KATHLEEN STEINHAUER came
home from residential school as full members of Saddle Lake Cree
Nation. As they entered adulthood, their band membership and
treaty rights were never in question. Falling in love and marrying
would change everything.

◆ Nellie Carlson

In 1945, at the age of eighteen, Nellie Makokis returned to the Saddle
Lake reserve to work. "I met my uncle, George Hunter, in St. Paul,"
[the nearby town] she recalled. "He thought he could keep an eye on
me. I took care of his kids, two boys and a girl. They were Catholics,
and I was Protestant. I also did farm work, feeding the pigs, milking
the cows. He lived on the edge of the Saddle Lake reserve at St. Bride's,
on the part of the reserve that had been sold. Six-mile corner."

Nellie Makokis at sixteen (right), with her older sister Ruth Makokis Maziarka, twenty-two.

For entertainment, Nellie loved to go to community dances. "I never smoked or drank. I loved dancing! That was my vice. I went out with boys, and none of them could dance. Jean-Marie Cardinal used to play the fiddle at the dances, and he would pick me up with his horses and wagon on the way."

Nellie's father had died during her childhood. Five years later, her mother Marjorie married into the Shirt family. While visiting at the home of her relatives Ralph and Edna Shirt, Nellie met Edna's brother, a returning war veteran who had come to live at Saddle Lake. His name was Elmer Carlson. Nellie and Elmer got married on June 12, 1947.

Despite his Swedish surname, Elmer has belonged to the Cree community from birth and continues to speak fluent Cree. He was a direct descendant of the Cree chief Kehewin, who signed Treaty Six. Born in rural Alberta on October 7, 1924, Elmer spent his earliest

Elmer Carlson moved to Saddle Lake after serving in the Canadian Army during the Second World War. There he met Nellie Makokis, and they married on June 12, 1947.

years with family members on the Kehewin Cree Nation reserve. Elmer's father, August Carlson, was a man of Swedish descent but Elmer didn't know him well as a child. His mother, born Helen Waskewitch, was a Cree woman with treaty status, a daughter of a chief, Sam Waskewitch and his first wife Sara, and a great-granddaughter of Kehewin. Helen had married twice, and had eight children altogether, five of whom survived to adulthood. Throughout her long life, she refused to give up her treaty rights. "Years ago, the Indian Agent would just sign women out when they got married,"

Elmer explained. "She would say, 'My Dad used to be a chief at Kehewin reserve.'[1] She refused to sign any papers they put before her....The RCMP came to their house in Holden. Her husband would take her to Onion Lake reserve [to settle the matter of her treaty status, at the insistence of the government Indian Agent.] She would say, 'The chiefs would make a good fire with these papers.'" While Helen stood firm, she could not obtain treaty rights for her children who had no Indian status after her marriages.

As a toddler and young child, Elmer lived entirely with his Cree relations. One day when he was seven years old, an older brother came to the Kehewin reserve to take him to Onion Lake Residential School. He stayed in the residential school, as a student, and later as an employee, until he was eighteen. With the Second World War in its third year, he travelled to Regina to join the army. "A lot of people will say they signed up because it was the patriotic thing to do," he recalled. "I signed up because I wanted to see the country and the world. War is not a pleasant thing but I did get a chance to travel to new places." Elmer trained in Ontario and at Yarmouth in Nova Scotia before he was shipped overseas. Assigned to the Lake Superior Regiment, he trained in England for nine months and served in France, Holland, Belgium and Germany. "At the very end of the war, about a week before it ended, I was wounded in Holland. I took a bullet through my neck, into my windpipe. I spent a little time in hospital, and then was shipped to England for an operation." He couldn't speak for a time, but recovered.

"I didn't get wounded that badly. I saw the country I enlisted to serve. I thought I had an easy time in the war. Some had it a lot worse. I was thankful I was coming home alive." Sometime during the war, his mother Helen, who had an alcohol problem, promised that she would quit drinking forever if he came back alive. By good fortune, he did. She kept her promise.

As a young couple, Nellie and Elmer Carlson moved away from the Saddle Lake reserve and never returned. Nellie describes the reasons vividly in the passages that follow. From 1947 until 1951, the

Helen Waskewitch Cardinal Carlson Memnook, mother-in-law of Nellie Carlson, was a great-granddaughter of Chief Kehewin, and refused to surrender her treaty rights after her marriages to men without treaty status, despite the efforts of the Department of Indian Affairs to take away those rights.

Department of Indian Affairs categorized women with treaty status who had married non-status or Métis men as "red-ticket holders." Nellie held a red ticket. In the *Indian Act* revisions of 1951, the federal government eliminated the treaty rights of red-ticket holders and their children and ruled that they could no longer live on reserves.[2] While chiefs and band councils discussed membership questions in meetings, and voted on some matters, they had no authority to oppose the government's *Indian Act* regulations. Individuals who criticized the rules stood a risk of being struck from the Band List if the Indian Agent considered them troublemakers. Nellie challenged the Indian Agent on the issue before her family's departure from the reserve.

Elmer found employment as an agricultural worker on a mixed farm in Riley, Alberta, and the Carlsons welcomed their first children in a home in nearby Tofield. The family moved to Edmonton after Elmer encountered a serious health crisis with cancer in his late thirties. He subsequently worked in maintenance at the Charles Camsell Hospital[3] in Edmonton to provide the family income.

Nellie says that her husband supported her work with Indian Rights for Indian Women, and shared her perspective on the destructive nature of the federal government's *Indian Act* and the importance of passing on the Cree culture and traditions to their children and grandchildren. Elmer was also proud of his own mother's effort to challenge the government's rules on membership in her own way.

Nellie Carlson on Marriage and the *Indian Act*

At first, after my marriage, I was what they called "a red-ticket holder." That was what the Department of Indian Affairs called us. It meant I had a treaty number, and I could live on a reserve, but I had no voice.

The rule about the red-ticket holder was passed in 1947. It meant that women who married non-status Indians or Métis or white men could live on the reserve and receive treaty annuities, but not all treaty rights.

The *Indian Act* section on women and marriage was changed six times over the years. On the sixth time, the women and their children lost all rights and were arbitrarily deleted from band membership lists. The changes were discussed between 1946 and 1950. At that time, many of my relatives—Ralph Steinhauer, George Hunter, Edward Cardinal—were on the band council at Saddle Lake. I remember two of them came to me and said: "The women lost." They voted against us, and allowed women of other races to remain as status Indians.

When I got married, though, we still had the red-ticket system. Treaty people would hold a white ticket: a man and his wife and children. Women who married non-status Indians would hold a red ticket. The Métis and non-status Indians would hold a blue ticket. A blue-ticket was not deemed to be an Indian; they could vote in national and provincial elections, and buy land and buy alcohol. But this system didn't last....In 1950–51, under the new revisions of the *Indian Act*, Section 12(1)(b), I lost my band membership and so did my children.

At one time, in the past, the Department of Indian Affairs didn't care too much about families that brought in newcomers and made them band members. In 1867, if you were a quarter Indian, you could be a status Indian. But by 1950, you could be a full-blooded Indian and lose treaty status—if you were a woman. White women could gain treaty rights for themselves and their children by marrying into the band. They have no right to Indian treaty rights. Elmer told me, "Don't be afraid to say that, because it's true." When we married, we automatically lost a land base.

Nellie's Promise

I had a kind mother. My uncle George Hunter came to me in 1950 to tell me she was dying. I went to see her. That's when my mother spoke to me about treaty rights, and also spoke to me about what would happen...

Marjorie Jackson Makokis Shirt,
the mother of Nellie Carlson,
in her youth.

My mother died in November 1950. Before she died, on her deathbed, she talked to me. And I have no witnesses because I was the only one there. When I went into her room, I was shocked when I looked at her. They had a low light by her head, like a night lamp, but she shone just like the holy pictures. She was just shining.... She beckoned me in. It scared me. I went to her bed. "This is my mother," I thought. "Why am I scared of her?" I guess she wanted to talk to me. So she said to me: "I want you to do something." I touched her legs, and they were as stiff as can be.

She said to me: "You are standing among the flowers, and these flowers, the petals, children's faces are among these flowers. Those babies whose eyes are open are already born. Those babies whose eyes are closed are not born yet." In Cree, these words sounded so nice. "These children do not know what will affect them when they come to this earth," she said. She kept talking. "Would you do something for them?"

She said to me: "Say yes."

Not knowing what I would have to do, I said yes.

She said: "You know people will not understand you but you're going to walk on this fine line. Promise me you will do this. So many Indian people are losing something....I wanted you to come here." She said: "People will never understand you. There will be heavy emotionalism." She didn't use the word hatred. But she said, "That's alright. You are doing that for the children. Do not be afraid." She was so tired after she said that.

Twelve days after she died, I suffered the same thing, a ruptured appendix. I was also in the hospital in St. Paul, very ill. There was this French lady there, another patient, who said to me in Cree: "I'll go, you stay." I didn't know why she said that. "I'll go, you stay." After that, the nurses came to get me and put me in a private room. That's when the doctor came in and said, "Are you a treaty Indian?" And I said, "Partially." And I said that in my wallet there was my treaty ID, and was he ever surprised when he read that policy that affected me because of marrying someone who was not a band member. He phoned Indian Affairs, and he said to me, "I'm going to operate on you immediately."

I think I had a near-death experience. I was looking down from above. I was out of my body, as I was being pushed to the operating room. "Wait," I remember saying to the nurses. I wanted to say goodbye to the other patients. All that time I was looking down from the ceiling. My husband came in. They put me out. That's all I remember. I went to a beautiful place, it seemed like it was so peaceful, so serene. Something like that went over me. And I was standing there, and then following my mother. I was trying to get to her, and she kept gesturing me to go back. I could see women walking around in dark circles. I could see my husband and another man and a priest praying at the foot of my bed.

All of a sudden I heard voices. I heard the doctor talking to my husband, saying, "Mr. Carlson, had I known you were willing to pay for her prescription I would have asked you to pay for it."

It seemed to me I went to heaven. I came back with a certain strength. I don't get hurt easily. I don't get depressed. I have this certain energy that I seem to spread so that everything around me goes well.

Nellie Leaves Saddle Lake

Kay used to ask me why I took myself off band membership at Saddle Lake. Here is the story.

When I had my appendix crisis as a young woman, Dr. Roland Decosse was my doctor in St. Paul. His father was French but his mother was Métis. I became very, very ill and needed medicine in the hospital. Dr. Decosse asked me if I was a treaty Indian, or a red-ticket person.[4] He called the Indian Agent. I could hear him yelling and screaming on the phone. No one argues with Indian Affairs, but they certainly open their eyes when a white person is yelling at them.

Dr. Decosse contacted the Department of Indian Affairs and arranged for me, a red-ticket holder, to be reinstated as a registered Indian just for my medical care, and also for my first two kids [born

Nellie and Elmer Carlson with their daughter Ruth.

Some of the Carlson children and a friend. Top, left to right: June; Ruth holding her young brother Gary; and Norma. Bottom, left to right: Pat Shirt and Gerald "Manny" Carlson. Altogether Nellie and Elmer Carlson had nine children, with two others dying in infancy.

before 1950], but my other kids had no rights at all. I couldn't argue with Indian Affairs, but a doctor could. If you fight hard enough with the Department of Indian Affairs and Medical Services Branch, they will back off. That experience gave me the picture. For us, though, you couldn't speak against the *Indian Act*. Those were the rules in those days.

Dr. Decosse told me before I left the hospital, "Mrs. Carlson, you have an interesting case." He warned me: "There is a clause in the *Indian Act* that says you cannot speak out against the *Indian Act*, or you can be taken off the Band List or prosecuted." He said: "You should fight for your Indian status because they are taking these rights away from you....You are entitled to education, health care rights, to whatever those men get."

I took myself off the Band List so I could speak against the *Indian Act*.

We women must have been strong to put up with that hassle. You know what? I am not going to say I'm proud. I will just say that I'm thankful that we were blessed with the energy that we used to correct this mess. I think it was a master plan by the government. They took so much land, all the land, gave Indian people some land base, but at the same time, not enough land base for future generations. And I always think: That's what we should have looked at. All of us Indian people, on-reserve and off-reserve. But there was this section in there. If you spoke against the *Indian Act*, you were prosecuted. In fact, that was what Mr. Knapp, the Indian Agent, told me when I came to say goodbye, when I took myself off the band membership list.

They didn't allow you to come in and see them. You had to stand at this window. When I went to see the Indian Agent, he sat behind a half-door, a sliding door, in his office. You never got a chance to talk to him up close. I unlocked the hook, and I went in. Uncle Ed caught up with me, and took my arm and said: "Don't go." But I went right in, and I said to the Indian Agent, "Sir, I came to say goodbye." He said, "Get this damn Indian woman out of here!" He just said that.

And I said right back to him: "See! You called me an Indian woman! That is what I am!" He didn't like to hear me saying that. We were expected to respect them. I guess we didn't! And I said, "I've come here to tell you. I'll be back to fight for my treaty rights." That's when he said: "Oh, no, you can't."

And I said: "I can!"

I went to pick up my money, and it was only $150. And then I just signed the paper. And the next day we left the reserve. I never looked back. I was never sorry. I was never depressed. Sure, I was feeling sorry for my kids. Had it not been for a government policy they would not be treated like this. And I felt sorry I was putting them into a white society with racism, but I wasn't sad for myself.

Elmer went to Edmonton, looking for work. A farmer from Riley came to the city looking for a good farm hand on a big farm, run by three brothers and an old man. We lived there for two or three years. One of the brothers moved away and we moved into his house at Tofield. When Elmer was thirty-eight he had a health crisis. He became very sick from pneumonia and went to the University of Alberta Hospital in Edmonton. A cancerous tumour was discovered in his lung. A surgeon from the veterans' hospital removed part of his right lung in difficult surgery.

I asked, "Will he be slowly getting better?" The doctor talked to me. Everyone around us was crying like heck, but I wasn't. Maybe I have no heart, but I was thinking: "He is the one who is suffering. Why would I cry for me?"

◆ Kathleen Steinhauer

Kathleen returned to Saddle Lake from her unhappy experience at residential school to study at home with her sisters for a time before pursuing her secondary studies in Edmonton. Later she discovered her lifelong vocation—nursing—and pursued a professional specialty in public health with higher education and jobs in other areas of Alberta.

Along the way she married her first husband, Allan Small Face, a member of the Kainai First Nation in the Treaty Seven territory in southern Alberta. They married on June 27, 1956 and had two sons, Davy, born July 8, 1958 at the Blood Indian Hospital in southern Alberta, and Mark, born on November 13, 1959 in a hospital in St. Paul, near the Saddle Lake reserve. As was the practice at the time, Kathleen's band membership was transferred from Saddle Lake Cree Nation to the Kainai First Nation, then known as the Blood tribe, immediately after her marriage.

In a short time the couple separated and Kathleen returned to her family roots in Saddle Lake to raise her children. She divorced Allan Small Face in February 1964. Kathleen was frustrated to learn that her band membership remained with the Blood tribe, although she would have preferred to return to the Saddle Lake Band List where she had family kinship and Cree cultural ties. She would eventually challenge the Department of Indian Affairs on this issue in a successful court case launched in 1992.[5] However, in the difficult intervening years, she would forfeit her treaty rights and band membership altogether—and all because she found the love of her life.

When Kathleen married Gilbert Anderson in the spring of 1965, she knew she would lose her treaty rights and band membership due the strict rules of the *Indian Act*, even though her new husband had a fair claim to registered Indian status. In the narrow legal definitions of the era, the federal government identified Gilbert as a "non-status Indian." He rejected that definition, in his daily life and in his long campaign to win full recognition for his disinherited First Nation.

Born in Calahoo, Alberta in 1934, Gilbert grew up just west of Edmonton on the Stony Plain Indian Reserve, home of the Enoch Cree Nation. As a child and teenager, he lived with his older half-brother Lawrence and quickly began to share his family's love of traditional music. Until he was in his early thirties, Gilbert played guitar for Lawrence and his brother Pete, both well-known fiddlers, at community dances and house parties at Enoch, and elsewhere.

Gilbert was a direct descendant of Chief Michel Callihoo, a Cree-Iroquois leader in Alberta who signed an adhesion to Treaty Six at Fort Edmonton in 1878 to bring the Michel band into treaty. He also had ancestors and family relations in the Papaschase Cree and the Enoch Cree Nations, as well as in the Métis community in the Edmonton area. His primary identification was always with the Michel First Nation.[6]

The story of the Michel First Nation begins with an adventurous voyageur, Louis Kwarakwante,[7] born on October 17, 1782 to Mohawk parents in Ganawake, near Montreal. When the eighteen-year-old signed his contract as a First Nations voyageur in 1800, the fur trade company clerk noted his surname as "Caliheue." The young man travelled west to work around Fort Augustus in the place we now know as Edmonton, and founded a large family with Cree and Sekani wives. They lived, worked and travelled through the Athabasca region, northern Rockies and around Fort Edmonton and Lac St. Anne. One of Louis's sons with his wife, Marie Patenaude, was Michel Callihoo, who also worked in the fur trade at Fort Edmonton. After he signed the adhesion to Treaty Six, bringing his band into treaty, Chief Michel Callihoo claimed a large reserve west of St. Albert where his extended family and their relations settled and prospered.

Like all First Nations in the Edmonton area, the Michel band members came under heavy government and settler pressure to surrender their rich agricultural land. Land sales marked by government corruption steadily eroded their land base through the next half-century. In 1958, the Michel band became the only First Nation in Canada in the twentieth century to enfranchise—dissolving its reserve and leaving treaty—under circumstances that many Michel members and descendants subsequently challenged. Without Ottawa's recognition, they reorganized as the Michel First Nation and launched a land claim in 1992 that remains unresolved.

Gilbert Anderson led this campaign as an early chief of the re-formed Michel First Nation in the 1990s. His quest for justice on the Michel case became a consuming interest. As Kathleen remembers, "Whenever anyone complained that Indians cost Canadian taxpayers a lot of money, he would say, 'It's a small price for a big land.'"

As a couple, Gilbert and Kathleen also became deeply involved in the renaissance of Cree-Métis cultural traditions in Edmonton, especially traditional fiddling and dancing. Later in life Gilbert became a respected fiddle teacher on northern Alberta's Métis settlements. The couple often performed together, with Gilbert on fiddle and Kathleen on piano, and they joined an influential early dance group to revive interest in authentic traditions. They also spoke to academic researchers interested in the cultural legacy of the Cree-Métis fur trade era, and Gilbert participated in the Northern Alberta Fiddle Project.[8]

Settling in Edmonton after their marriage, the couple raised their children Davy, Mark, Celina and Gilbert Jr. and actively participated in the cultural and political life of the urban Aboriginal community and the city at large. Gilbert worked as a federal and provincial civil servant to provide the family income. He supported Kathleen's activism in Indian Rights for Indian Women even though he doubted for many years that the movement would succeed.

Gilbert began a strenuous fight with cancer in the spring of 2010. The following spring his family and best friends gathered at his bedside in a palliative care centre as he enjoyed one last fiddle tune with them, *Cat Scratch Reel*. With their hearts breaking, Kathleen and her daughter Celina managed to dance together beside his bed. An hour later, on March 1, 2011, Gilbert Elzear Anderson died at the age of seventy-six. He and Kathleen had been married for forty-five years. A year later, shortly after a family gathering to mark the first anniversary of his passing, Kathleen died suddenly of heart failure on March 4, 2012.[9]

Although Gilbert had lived for most of his life without federal government recognition of his treaty or Aboriginal rights, he died with his full treaty rights restored—thanks to the strenuous efforts of women like Kathleen Steinhauer, Nellie Carlson and the other activists in the Indian Rights for Indian Women movement.

Kathleen Steinhauer on Marriage and the *Indian Act*

I came to Edmonton to finish my [secondary] studies. We took courses at Alberta College but had to finish Grade Twelve at Victoria High School because the college had discontinued some courses. I boarded at the residence of Alberta College, for $150 a month, with my sister Doreen. That's where I became friends with Pauline Gladstone[10] from the Blood reserve; she would eventually marry Hugh Dempsey[11] and have five kids. My other friend was Georgina Davis.

I worked as a ward aide at the Charles Camsell Hospital while I was in Grade Twelve, and after I graduated I applied to the Lamont Hospital for nursing training. I was three years in training, with two months at Ponoka and the Bowness TB sanitorium.

In 1954, I graduated from nursing school. I began to work at the Charles Camsell Hospital on the first of November. They were looking for Christmas relief nurses at the Blood Indian Hospital in Cardston. I thought I'd go. At the time, I was working on a ward at the Camsell with eighteen-month old kids, so cute. I worked with nurses' aides I knew from home, from Saddle Lake and Goodfish Lake [a reserve near Saddle Lake]. The kids developed infectious hepatitis, and a bunch of us got it. I got sick on my way to Cardston, and when I got there, instead of going to work, I was put in hospital for treatment. I was there for three weeks and home for three weeks on Workers' Compensation. I asked if I could go back.

I knew Jean Burgess, who had been at Saddle Lake, and Pauline Gladstone's parents, Jim and Jenny Gladstone. I also met the man who would become my first husband, Allan Small Face. His mother was a cook's helper at the hospital; his aunt was a cook. I became friends with his sister, Marie.[12]

The hospital at Cardston was at the edge of the reserve, and very small. It was across the road from the "white hospital"—well, that's what we called it. I made friends on the reserve. One young woman wanted to go to the beer parlour to see if she'd be kicked out as a treaty Indian. I went along but I didn't even finish my beer. It tasted

Above: Kathleen Steinhauer receives top award in Grade Eleven, Alberta College, Edmonton, 1950.
Right: Kathleen Steinhauer, graduate nurse, 1954.

awful. The others weren't Indian girls, but white. One of my friends, Pam Shackleford, was an English girl working at the hospital. She said, "Come to England." I had attended the Canadian Nurses Association meeting in Quebec City and I was hooked on travel, so I agreed.

By this time I was twenty-four years old. This was a couple years after graduation, in 1956. I booked passage on an ocean liner but decided to fly TCA instead. I spent three weeks with Pam's family and worked as a nanny for an English family with twins. They took me everywhere, Buckingham Palace, all the places you can see in six months. It rained all the time. I saw mother's cousins in Glasgow. I just loved England with a purple passion.

Allan Small Face had signed up with the Canadian Forces, and he was serving with the Princess Pats in Germany. He came back to England and stayed. Like a silly fool, I married him.... Pam Shackleford, my friend, was very doubtful. I married Allan in June. His posting was nearly finished; he'd served his three years. In October or November I came back to Canada, alone, to settle in Cardston. I liked the people there. I got along very well with everyone. By May Allan was back on the Blood reserve. My first son Davy was born in the summer of 1958.

I worked as a school nurse at the residential school after Davy was born. It was St. Paul's Residential School, with Father de Woolf as principal. This was an Anglican school for children from the Blood reserve. The principal often said derogatory things about the students, calling them dumbies. I bawled him out. I said he was not to call them that anymore. It was demeaning. That was the beginning of the end of my career there.

At the residential school, the sewers backed up. The kids were always sick; the undernourishment was dreadful. Mac and cheese, mac and cheese. No fruit, very few vegetables. The kids were always hacking and coughing. I complained about this. Father de Woolf said, "Write me a report in two weeks," so I did. The secretary read it and typed it for me. I took it to him. He said to me: "I never asked for that. I didn't want it." And I was so angry I threw it in the waste-paper basket. But someone else must have complained too. Lyman Jampolsky was a principal at Cardston High School, and he was aware of the condition of the residential school as some students from the reserve attended his school and talked about it. Lyman had grown up in Spedden, near Saddle Lake, and the kids liked him. He was fed up [with the state of the residential school]. A committee was formed, with the Department of Indian Affairs, the superintendent of schools and Lyman. Ruby, the secretary, saw their report dealing with racism and poor education but with health problems as well. She told me: "All the things you put in your report were in there, too."

I was the senior girls' supervisor and nurse. I was teaching the senior girls First Aid and helping with the girls' bugle band, taking lessons with them every week. Mr. De Woolf was going to cut our pay, from $175 a month, down $75. I objected to this. I was a trouble-maker right from the start.

I began to have problems with my marriage. When I became pregnant again, I packed up, called Mum, and said: "I'm coming home." I had my second son, Mark, in St. Paul after I left the Blood reserve with Davy. I was always advised, "Don't sign any documents that Indian Affairs sends you related to the boys." I knew that what-ever they sent, I was not going to sign it because they were entitled to the treaty status they were born with.

My Dad and my Mum were very supportive when I left my first husband. They had come to see me in Cardston and said: "You come home if you need to." But later when I tried to get my band membership and treaty rights back at Saddle Lake, now that was a totally different thing. I used to say: "Why do you make a difference with this?" They just did. My Dad used to say: "Nobody will take my treaty rights away from me, sweetheart." Well why should I be any different?

The move out of my marriage turned out for the best. I felt inade-quate, like a failure, but that was wrong. I had a lot of family support.

When my marriage dissolved, I went straight back to Saddle Lake. That was my home! I went to work in the public health unit in St. Paul near Saddle Lake reserve.

My Auntie Marie Steinhauer, married to my grandfather's brother Harrison, came and lived with me in St. Paul to help with the children. She was a profound and awesome help to me as well as a jolly person. She always hummed hymns while she worked, and lived to be ninety-two or ninety-three. She was kindly to Davy and Mark, and I appreciated her. I went to work in the health unit in the summer of 1960, and then in the fall went to the university during the winter for public health training. Auntie Marie would make fresh bread and bannock for the boys, and she planted a garden for us in the spring. In 1961 she decided to take the summer off and recommended I hire Lillian Shirt from Saddle Lake, which I did. My sister June and Cecile Dion also helped with the children while I was working. My community in my childhood and at this time was Saddle Lake.

My Dad was appointed to Canada's Centennial Commission in 1963, the token Indian I presume. My Mum and Dad travelled all over Canada. I remember they bought a sealskin coat for my mother in Inuvik. This experience was good for my Dad, but my mum didn't always like the travelling. In Halifax, they happened to meet Mr. De Woolf. He said to them: "We really missed your daughter when she left our school. What an asset she was!" And what a hypocrite he was!

Back in Saddle Lake, I worked in the Northeastern Alberta Health Unit in St. Paul. I decided to apply to the University of Alberta to study for a diploma in public health. I attended the university from September to April 1961, and graduated. I did my field training in Cranbrook, BC. My mum took care of my two little kids while I was away.

I found a job with the Leduc Strathcona Health Unit [near Edmonton]. Wally Waltzer was moving to Edmonton from Saddle Lake with his family to take teacher training. I rented a suite in their basement, a good arrangement. They needed the money, and I needed a place to live. After I arrived I phoned the five or six people I knew in Edmonton. Phil Thompson took me to the Canadian Native

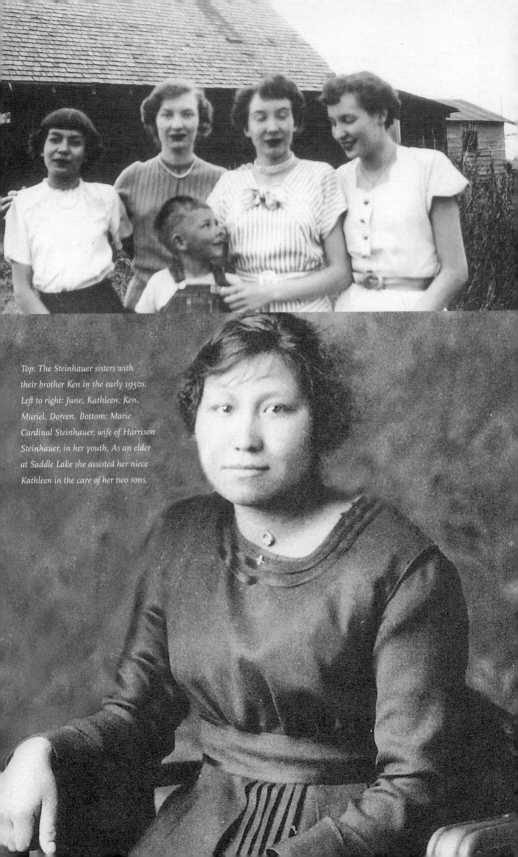

Top: The Steinhauer sisters with their brother Ken in the early 1950s. Left to right: June, Kathleen, Ken, Muriel, Doreen. Bottom: Marie Cardinal Steinhauer, wife of Harrison Steinhauer, in her youth. As an elder at Saddle Lake she assisted her niece Kathleen in the care of her two sons.

Gilbert Anderson, a direct descendant of Chief Michel Callihoo, led the Michel band's struggle for federal recognition for many years.

Kathleen Steinhauer married Gilbert Anderson on June 27, 1965.

Friendship Centre for the first time. He was an executive director there. I went to hang around the Friendship Centre after that, and met many people. At the time it was located at the corner of 108th Street and 101st Avenue in an old house, where CJCA used to be.

Eugene Steinhauer,[13] my cousin, was in town at that time. My Dad said he'd be coming home for Christmas, and I could get a ride with him. I didn't want to go home alone on winter roads. It was very cold, a snowstorm. Eugene and Lucas Redcrow and Billy Halfe came over. We stuffed blankets into the old car, and it was so cold. We picked up Alex Janvier[14] on the way. It took us five hours to get home in the blizzard.

When we came back to Edmonton after Christmas, Eugene invited me to a party at the Friendship Centre. It was his first AA birthday, and he invited me to this anniversary of his sobriety. We were cousins; we had grown up together. I was so proud of him. He introduced me to a bunch of people, including Gilbert Anderson and Maria Campbell.[15] Later at the party I noticed this guy looking at me from a window. Our eyes met. He drew back right away. The next week I got a call from Eugene. "Do you remember Gilbert Anderson? Would you like to go to a dance?" I told him I'd love to go to a dance if there was no drinking. "I don't mind third-wheeling," I said. "I've been doing that for a long time." He put Gilbert on the line, and I couldn't remember this guy! *[Laughing.]* He asked if I'd like to go with him. It was like a blind date. Mike Steinhauer, Eugene's brother, was there, too.

I wore a very conservative dress. Gilbert came by in his jeans with a V-neck cardigan. Then I remembered. He was the guy gawking at me through the window. On the way the headlights went out in his car, and he got out and kicked the fender. I was dying to laugh but I had to be careful. I had a really good time. These dances were fun, and there was no drinking. I liked to meet people in a healthy atmosphere. Big Miller, the black jazz musician, was playing sax. Then Alphonse Thomas from Enoch reserve came into the room. I knew him, and he came to speak to me. He said, "I have to speak to Gilbert to tell him his brother Pete has died." It was leukemia, and expected, but still a terrible shock. "Wait fifteen minutes," I said. I wanted him to have a few more happy moments. When I went to get my coat, I could see them talking.

I didn't want to get married at first. I didn't want to lose my treaty rights. Gilbert had as much Aboriginal ancestry as me, through the Michel band and the Enoch Cree, but his family had lost treaty rights through the years. I knew my children needed a dad. And Gilbert would say to me: "Do you love me enough to get married and lose your treaty rights?" And I would always say: "I am going to get my treaty rights back!"

My sisters lost their band membership through marriage, too. Muriel married Peter Manywounds from Sarcee [now the Tsuu T'ina First Nation] and lost her Saddle Lake membership. Doreen and June married white men and lost their rights altogether. The government

found all kinds of excuses to take people off the treaty Band Lists....
As Gilbert says, whoever is in charge closes his eyes and throws a
dart, and that's who you are.

I remember Gilbert saying to me, "You would give up your treaty
rights to get married?" And I said: "Never mind. I'll get them back."
And Gilbert said, "Oh, forget about it. You'll never get your treaty
rights." And I pounded the table. I was really angry, and he knew it.
And I said: "I'll get my rights and you'll get your rights and our children will get their rights." He put on his jacket, and I said after him,
"and all our descendants!" His attitude changed when the law was
changed, when he and other men got their treaty status back, too...

maskawâtisiwin / strength of character 4

Indian Rights for Indian Women

IN THE LATE 1960S, the First Nations, Métis and Inuit peoples of Canada entered a decade of intense political organization and activism. They invented new political organizations, and revived older ones. They researched historic injustices against their communities, filed land and treaty claims, and launched lawsuits against the federal government. They marched in protest demonstrations against racism, and in particular against Canada's stated plan in the White Paper of 1969 to end the collective rights and special status promised to the First Nations in the treaties. Harold Cardinal and the Alberta chiefs led national opposition to this scheme, expressed in their own document, *Citizens Plus*, usually referred to as the Red Paper. It began with strong words: "For us who are treaty Indians, there is nothing more important than our treaties, our lands and the well-being of future generations." The federal government withdrew its plan in 1971.

Other leaders challenged the oppressive rules of the Department of Indian and Northern Affairs, and a century-old *Indian Act*, in every possible way they could manage. In the Northwest Territories, Dene and Métis elders stood in line with younger activists to tell Justice Thomas Berger why the Mackenzie Valley pipeline could not be built without their consent. Maria Campbell, Harold Cardinal, and Howard Adams wrote best-selling books that challenged the smug Canadian assumption that civil rights struggles happened only south of the border. The imposed silence of the 1950s, the fear of speaking out against the Indian Agent, was over in Canada. The new generation had no fear.

In this lively atmosphere, disinherited First Nations women across the country demanded an end to the sexual discrimination in the membership rules of the *Indian Act*. They began to organize, almost simultaneously, in cities and towns across the country. The Women's Liberation Movement had been gaining strength among feminists around the globe, and here in Canada, the 1970 Royal Commission on the Status of Women reported a deep national desire among women for full equal rights. Like many First Nations women, Nellie Carlson and Kathleen Steinhauer focused on their battle with the Government of Canada and its discriminatory *Indian Act*. They organized an ad hoc group in Alberta, and reached out for allies.

Far from the prairies, a Mohawk woman from Kahnawake in Quebec offered the Alberta women her strong support and friendship. Mary Two-Axe Earley had also lost Indian treaty status when she married an Irish-American electrical engineer in New York. In 1966, Mary held a Mohawk friend of hers in her arms as she died. Her friend had also lost her band membership after marrying a Mohawk man from a different community; she had been ordered to sell her house and leave the reserve. Mary was convinced that the woman had died of a heart attack as a result of this severe stress, and she was furious that her friend could not be buried at Kahnawake. She decided to act.

Mary founded Equal Rights for Indian Women as a provincial organization in Quebec in 1967, and this organization soon became part of the nation-wide Indian Rights for Indian Women. She began to work with Jenny Shirt Margetts in Alberta, who became co-president, and with other disinherited women from across the country. They later expanded the group to a national organization. In 1969, after her husband's death, Mary moved back to a house in Kahnawake that she had inherited from her grandmother. To stay on the reserve, she gave the house to her daughter who had married a Mohawk man—but she lived in it too. The Kahnawake band council used the *Indian Act* to evict her in 1975, and gave her sixty days to move off the reserve. The eviction notice was eventually withdrawn, but it underlined the urgency of the Indian Rights for Indian Women campaign.

When Mary asked permission to speak to the prime minister and premiers about *Indian Act* discrimination at a 1983 conference, and was refused, former Quebec premier René Lévesque gave her his chair at the first ministers' meeting. Her words to them were clear: "Please search your hearts and minds, follow the dictates of your conscience, set my sisters free."

Her sisters in Alberta worked beside her every step of the way.

For Nellie Carlson and Kathleen Steinhauer, the 1970s opened as an exciting decade of hard work and urban activism. Along with Jenny Margetts, they knew most of the male activists from the Indian Association of Alberta and the Métis Association of Alberta—Harold Cardinal,[1] Stan Daniels,[2] and Harry Daniels,[3] among many others—and they began vigorous debates with them about sexual discrimination. Eugene Steinhauer, a founder of the Alberta Native Communications Society, and subsequently a president of the Indian Association of Alberta, was a cousin from Saddle Lake. Gilbert Anderson, Kathleen's husband, began a long battle for redress for the disbanded Michel First Nation. Descendants of the Papaschase band in Edmonton began a similar struggle using the archival research they obtained from Kathleen. The Canadian Native Friendship Centre in Edmonton, originally organized as an urban welcome centre, became a place of social action, practical anti-poverty work and political discussion.

◆ Nellie Carlson

We were a group of women who worked to end Section 12(1)(b), the discriminatory part of the *Indian Act* under a colonial system. The law said this: If any woman married a non-Indian—and that could be a non-status or Métis man—she and her children and descendants would lose their treaty rights, including the right to live on a reserve. But that didn't happen to men. They could marry anyone they liked, including a white woman, and she would gain Indian status and so would her children.

It wasn't fair. We were born and raised on the reserve with treaty rights under Treaty Six, which our ancestors signed in 1876. In the first *Indian Act*, it states that an Indian is a male. That meant that women were not even recognized as people! The people responsible for the Department of Indian Affairs in the early years had one purpose. Duncan Scott said: "We will work to see to it that one day not one Indian is left."[4] And so Section 12(1)(b) was one way that the Government of Canada used to assimilate people with treaty rights and eliminate their legal rights.

We created an organization called Indian Rights For Indian Women. People now have to understand what we were doing. They are not really thinking about how that law has affected them. It has affected most Aboriginal families across Canada: their sisters, mothers, aunts and cousins.

◆ Kathleen Steinhauer

Sometimes, in earlier times, even under the *Indian Act*, bands brought in non-status men and boys as band members—for example as informally adopted family members. And yet women born on the reserve would lose their status and right to live on the reserve as band members after marriage, and so would their children. It always angered us.

We were also concerned about men losing treaty rights in different ways. This is important. It needs to go into our book. One way that many treaty families lost their treaty rights was through military service. When the soldiers came home from the war, the government or Indian Agent said to them: "Sign these papers" and they had to sign or they wouldn't get their allotment [of benefits from the Department of Veterans Affairs, including land benefits]. Many treaty men were enfranchised after military service. So some of the treaty men were put off the membership lists, while newcomers, sometimes war brides from England, were put on the lists.

Many non-status Indians also lost status through odd and unfair circumstances. For example, one man I knew came back from the army. He had a shack, a house that belonged to his uncle and father. It was surveyed, and the Indian Agent said he would be relocated. He complained about this and they took him off band membership. This is when he lost treaty status. That happened in 1951.

◆ The Beginning of Indian Rights for Indian Women in Alberta

KATHLEEN: I remember I was sitting and talking with Lloyd Auger from Saddle Lake. This was in the late 1960s. I was complaining bitterly about the loss of treaty rights. He had lost his treaty rights when his mother married a non-status Indian. He said to me, "There's a woman around Toronto. She's really hot on this subject. Her name is Jeannette Corbière Lavell."[5] He gave us her address in Toronto. This was before 1969. He said, "She is very strongly opposed to Section 12(1)(b)." I asked him, "How do I get in touch with Jeannette?" He said he thought she was on Manitoulin Island, but he didn't know.

I began to think about Jeannette Corbière Lavell and other people who would join us. I knew Jean Cuthand was outspoken. I knew Marie Small Face Marule was very concerned about this. I wrote three letters to these women. Jean Cuthand wrote a very supportive letter in response but then she turned on us later. She did all kinds of things within the Secretary of State's office to retard the growth of our organization. After we met Jeannette Corbière Lavell, we found out that she had never received my letter. Marie didn't answer my letter. I was very disappointed.

Then one day Marie rang up and said: "Call your women together. I'm coming to Edmonton." So I called Nellie and Nellie phoned Jenny Margetts and Myrtle Calahasen. We met here, and sat around this table. Gordon Margetts, Jenny's husband, was here. Some guys came here to listen. Marie was very supportive. She got us started. "This is what you must do," she said. She wrote it all down for us, the legal resolutions, all of it. And we were off.

Marie Small Face Marule was the youngest sister of a man I had married when I was younger—my first husband, Allan Small Face. She was a member of the Blood tribe in southern Alberta, and she had studied anthropology or sociology for four years, and joined CUSO as a volunteer to teach in Zambia in the early 1960s. They told her before she left Canada that she would be considered white over there. They had a moped over there, and were driving on a trail, and she got into a serious accident. She was hospitalized in Zambia for six to eight weeks in Lusaka. While she was away from Canada, she married Jacob Marule. He was a freedom fighter in South Africa, a refugee from apartheid, who had been educated in Sweden. They split up, and Marie came back to stay in Canada.

Maria's dream was always to keep her treaty rights. The Blood band council wanted to take her off the Band List. She said, "Well, how do you know I'm married?" You see, the papers, the marriage documents, were in Zambia.

After I moved to Edmonton, we saw a lot of each other, and we talked about the issue. She was going to the University of Alberta and I was working at the Leduc Strathcona Health Unit. Later, when I wrote the letter, she was working for the National Indian Brotherhood in Ottawa as executive director; the president was George Manuel at that time. I wrote to her when she was in this capacity.

Marie was with us right at the beginning. If it hadn't been for her, we wouldn't have known how to proceed. She got into an awful tangle once the National Indian Brotherhood[6] turned against us, but I am grateful to her. We were totally ignorant of the civil procedures to follow. When Marie came to Edmonton that first time, we got organized. She knew what to do. We called ourselves, The Ad Hoc Committee on Indian Women's Rights. We wanted to deal with this issue, anybody and everybody, a good many students, social activists, Aboriginal women—we all wanted the repeal of Section 12(1)(b). Marie wrote out a business plan: what to do, when to do it and who to contact. All of this, she wrote on a piece of paper, on the back of our resolutions. She said one of the things you'll have to do is to go after them for your share of band assets.

We learned a lot. We went to a lot of organizations at the time, asking them to pass a resolution to support us.

NELLIE: Our true work began when the Secretary of State's office in Ottawa gave the Voice of Alberta Native Women a bit of money to prepare a presentation on foster care to the province. A staff member there told us to keep whatever was left over, and he encouraged us to hold a conference.

The Voice of Alberta Native Women Conference, Edmonton, 1968

NELLIE: At that time the Jeannette Corbière Lavell case was in the news. The Alberta women had $8,000 from the Secretary of State, and $1000 from the city and province, to hold this conference. Women in BC heard about it, and they wanted to come. Some women came from Ontario, Thunder Bay, and some from Nova Scotia. This was one of the first national meetings of First Nations and Métis women on this issue; we were the first conference, I think, to hold a Round Dance and a traditional feast. We could not pay mileage for these people, but we paid for bus tickets. We had no agenda to start with. We thought the confer-

ence would be about childcare and native children in foster care.

Jeannette Corbière Lavell's case came into the picture because she had won a challenge in the Ontario court. At the conference, a woman from Slave Lake stood up and said: "I have two daughters who have married off-reserve, and one has a husband in jail." She and her daughters could not return to their reserve although they wanted to. She put a motion on the floor that we deal with a reso-lution on Section 12(1)(b) of the *Indian Act*.

People from the Indian Association of Alberta told the women to stop it, not to deal with it. But Jenny Margetts seconded the motion. She said: "We have too many blue-eyed blonde women on the reserve claiming Indian status because they married Indian men." And she said there were too many Indian women and chil-dren pushed off the reserve and stripped of treaty rights because they marry non-status Indians, Métis or white men. Marguerite Ritchie, a non-Aboriginal lawyer from Ottawa, chaired our debate, to give even time to everyone. You could feel the tension building in that room. We talked about it all afternoon. It was decided to have our next meeting in March in Saskatoon.

The Meeting in Saskatoon

NELLIE: I had pneumonia and couldn't go to this meeting. I was in the hospital.

KATHLEEN: The Voice of Alberta Indian Women, that group, and other women's organizations seemed to me to be homemakers' clubs, full of sewing and baking, promoting home economics. I would never go to a meeting for that. I'd be bored silly. I was not interested in joining a women's organization at first. I thought they would be all about bake sales and that sort of thing. I didn't want to spend my energy on raffles and bake sales.

But I went to Saskatoon. Marie [Small Face Marule] had phoned Jeannette Corbière Lavell in Ontario. There were people there from Goodfish Lake, from reserves in Saskatchewan, and many were opposed to the women's case. You could feel the air getting more and more electric...

The opposition voices increased. Jean Goodwill was courageous enough to make a motion that the issue should be the main issue of this conference. Jean Goodwill was not an Indian Rights for Indian Women supporter later, but did make this effort at the meeting. And Monica Turner had the courage to stand up and say: "We will move to Room 1213 to continue this discussion." And then, by coincidence, thirteen women stood up and left the room. The thirteen women included: Mary Two-Axe Earley from Kahnawake, Marie Small Face Marule, Philomena Ross, Frieda Patiel, Jenny Margetts, Mary Louise Frying Pan, Philomena Aulotte, Ethel Johnson, Monica Turner, me, and three others.

We were thirteen women in Room 1213 on March 13, 1968. We always said that thirteen was our lucky number.

NELLIE: We didn't have a president, a secretary, a treasurer or a red cent. We named Monica Turner the eastern president, and Jenny Margetts the western president.[7]

KATHLEEN: We didn't have a name yet. I think we called ourselves Equality for Indian Women.

The Next Meeting of the Voice of Alberta Native Women, at the Canadian Native Friendship Centre in Edmonton

KATHLEEN: The conflict arose again when we returned to Edmonton. We brought the issue back to the Voice of Alberta Native Women Association. Bertha Clark was president. Rose Yellowfeet was vice-president. Nellie said she thought it was clear to everyone that the *Indian Act* discrimination would be on the agenda.

NELLIE: But the next morning it was off the agenda again, and they were back to talking about bake sales and rodeos. Bertha said: "Nellie, you must understand that this is not the appropriate place for this discussion." Jenny Margetts and I were coming up the stairs and I asked them: "How come you took it off the agenda?" And they said: "Out of respect to those [white women] who had treaty rights, we aren't going to deal with it." They didn't want to support us. And Jenny said, "Nellie, let's go downstairs and we'll organize our own group."

The Voice of Alberta Native Women? Chicken, chicken, chicken. The president didn't have the guts to stand up and talk about it. They were direct. They absolutely turned us down.

Jenny said, "Let's go downstairs and create an Ad Hoc Committee on the Status of Indian Women."[8] On the first evening, many treaty Indians were in favour of the women keeping their treaty rights when they married. The women who supported us were Mary Louise Frying Pan of Frog Lake, Philomena Ross, originally from Hobbema, and Philomena Aulotte from Onion Lake, originally.

KATHLEEN: All of this discussion was happening at that time due to the Jeannette Corbière Lavell case in the Ontario courts, and also because of the media attention to the Royal Commission on the Status of Women. Florence Bird, the Commission chair, had held hearings for six months across the country. She had given special attention to discrimination against Aboriginal women, and the report had recommended that Section 12(1)(b) be eliminated from the *Indian Act*.

Across the country, Mary Two-Axe Earley spoke about this issue. She had a friend from Kahnawake, a woman named Florence, who had married off their reserve, and died in Mary's arms in New York. She couldn't be buried on the reserve, and the land left to her by her parents could not go to her children. This is one thing that Mary had never forgotten.

NELLIE: Marie [Small Face Marule] told us at one point that the National Indian Brotherhood, where she worked, would advocate

Nellie Carlson (left) and Mary Two-Axe Earley at a meeting in Edmonton.

on our behalf. There was no way anybody was going to advocate for us. We will do the work, we said. And we were not doing it for ourselves, but for the sake of our children.

We gathered names at the Friendship Centre. We got bawled out by some people there, but we did get some support just the same. We began to hear from opponents that if we questioned Section 12(1)(b) then we would wreck the treaties and there would be no more reserves. Those who opposed us were so rude. They tried to intimidate us.

KATHLEEN: We were hard-up. We had no money to put into an organization, or lobbying or conferences....We didn't have a lot of

money for anything. What we had just came from family allowance cheques. We bought stamps, envelopes, and paper. We would sit together and compose what we wanted to say. We did better and better every year. We found names and addresses of new people to approach with our cause. We always sent copies of our letters to the National Indian Brotherhood and other organizations. In those years they would never reply.

NELLIE: The long-distance phone calls were always on me. My husband gave me money for this.

KATHLEEN: What were our early meetings like? Chaotic! We all had children. Sometimes we couldn't get a babysitter. Our kids would play as we talked and talked about Section 12(1)(b). They were bored to death.

The women who were the most hostile to us and to our cause had married into band membership. They would give us dirty looks, and they would cross the street to avoid us. The women who had married into the band from the outside and received treaty rights felt threatened. My own mother was against us. Many well-known Cree women were against us too. Helen Gladue. Agnes Bull. But we were heirs to the treaties, too.

NELLIE: A white woman, the wife of an Anglican minister, stood up at one meeting and talked about this issue. I said, "I don't want any more white people standing up and speaking on behalf of Indian people." It turned out this woman was a status Indian. She had treaty rights.

Gordon Margetts, Jenny's husband, took us to a meeting in Vancouver. Paul Jensen, a white sociologist who worked for the Indian Association of Alberta, helped us to rewrite revisions of the *Indian Act*. Harold Cardinal was there. The leaders, they stood at each mic, and did they ever bawl us out. Our friend Jim Robb, a law student at the University of Alberta, he was walking up and down, with his hands back behind him. Gordon said: "I would never have believed it if I hadn't been there."

We stood up to this guy. We twisted that paper, the *Indian Act*. After that a lot of people wouldn't speak to us. They would cross the street to avoid us. They felt as strongly about this issue as we did, only on the other side of it. People in our own families would say: "You're going to destroy the treaties. The reserves are going to fall apart." Also they kept telling us: "You made your choice when you married. You made your bed and now you must lie in it." Their position was that this was the natural way, to follow your husband. I remember Mary Anne Lavalee saying: "When you take your marriage vow, do you say, 'I promise to love, honour and obey on or off the reserve?'"

I never openly quarrelled with any of them. I just stated my position and left it at that. I did have an argument with Ralph Shirt. This was so unexpected. Ralph Shirt said: "You and Jenny Margetts are breaking up our treaty rights." And I said to him: "As I recall, Ralph, you were one of the band councillors in 1947 when the reserve land was sold....Your father sold part of the land at Saddle Lake. What about him? We are trying to make Indian rights strong, so that all Indian people, all descendants of the treaty signers, will have treaty rights."

And I said to him: "You sold your own daughters, and me, down the river. You supported white women's rights, and we didn't even have a drop of white man's blood." And I said to him: "I'm a full-blooded Indian."

At that time, our grandfathers, our grandmothers, punished me for speaking out. That same night I got into a serious car accident. Jenny and Lillian came to see me in the hospital. When Jenny came to see me, they were crying. I had broken wrists. I couldn't even eat my soup. "Quit crying!" I said. "Feed me my soup!" *[She laughs.]* I cleansed myself after speaking out. I felt so good for speaking.

KATHLEEN: Our organization, Indian Rights for Indian Women, was not organized across Canada like the Native Women of

Canada. Instead, the group had members and activists in different communities across the country. These women became friends across tribal lines and communicated by phone and letter, and worked together. Eventually the National Committee of Indian Rights for Indian Women was registered as an association. The Native Women's Association of Canada and other women's organizations always wanted us to expand our focus to foster care and other issues.

NELLIE: We would say, "No. That's important, but our issue is Section 12(1)(b) of the *Indian Act*. We're not talking about foster care or anything else. We want to talk about discrimination."

To get federal funding from the Secretary of State, any native women's organization had to have status and non-status members. I think they thought it would defeat us. But that's when we got the treaty people on board. Some women who were against us came to our meetings. They were very interested in learning. Some would say: "It is only you, the women affected, who will be able to make this change. I cannot say you are victims. I can say I admire you for standing up for your position."

KATHLEEN: We also protested other discrimination against Aboriginal women. There was this terrible song on the radio at the time. I remember it had the line "Squaws along the Yukon were good enough for me." Jenny Margetts seconded a motion by Yukon women to boycott radio stations that played that song, and we sent that resolution to Parliament.[9]

NELLIE: We phoned radio stations and told them not to play it anymore. The Yukon women asked for a resolution, and we supported it. This conference was held in December for the Indian Rights for Indian Women national committee. By coincidence, all leaders came there, so we tried to help them.

KATHLEEN: My father opposed the position of Indian Rights for Indian Women, and my mother supported him. I challenged him directly one time.

I had found a story at the back of the *Edmonton Journal* about the Jeannette Corbière Lavell case.[10] My parents were visiting, and I showed it to them. I was so surprised at the hostility I met. I put my hands on my father's shoulder and I said to him: "Don't you think my Indian husband has more right to treaty rights than your white wife?" That stopped them cold. There was silence after that.

They didn't talk to me for a long, long time. Doreen, my sister, called me and said, "You didn't need to be so nasty." But I thought it was a good argument, and it was. How many people were in our situation? I don't know why just the women lost their rights....My mother eventually supported us, and I think she convinced my Dad. However we very seldom argued about this issue with our families.

NELLIE: It was amazing how many people tried to distract us. So many of the male leaders and chiefs were hypocritical about us. Once I talked with Harold Cardinal about Section 12(1)(b). I said: "You know we're right." And he said: "Yes, I know, but my constituents don't know." We had long talks about the issue in Cree. He was always respectful.

KATHLEEN: Some men agreed with us quietly, we know they did. Men like Gordon Lee of Hobbema[11] and Mike Steinhauer at Saddle Lake. They understood the issues of treaty rights. But the Indian Association of Alberta absolutely refused to support us. Even my Dad said: "The women knew what they were doing when they married out." That made me furious. We heard privately that many men agreed with us. For example, John Maclean from Sturgeon Lake. He had many daughters. These men would speak publicly against us, but privately we knew many understood and sympathized with our situation.

NELLIE: My daughter was working for the Indian Association of Alberta, and someone asked her to pass on a message to me to quit my work in Indian Rights for Indian Women. I told her: "No young punk tells me what to do!"

Some people would talk to us in private, after meetings. One person said: "I am so proud of you. Never quit. I am so happy to see you are doing the right thing." But many other people with treaty status opposed us. When they see you, they just turn around. Nobody wants to talk to you. They make you feel like you are contaminating the air around them.

We knew about some IAA members, and other treaty people, who won treaty status due to adoption or other circumstances. For example Fred Gladstone's father had been brought into treaty status by the Bloods. I said to him: "Had it not been for the old people who brought your father in, you wouldn't have treaty status." And yet he opposed us. Some other men would make fun of what they called "squaw lib." Some men with treaty rights supported us and paid a price for it. The brother of Philomena Ross in Hobbema said "Listen to these women" and had his garage burned down...

KATHLEEN: Nellie and Philomena Ross were having lunch at the Friendship Centre one day, and Ralph Bouvette[12] saw them, and said: "Well here comes squaw lib." People laughed heartily. Ralph was a big man. Nellie took him by his necktie, pushed him against the wall and bawled him out in Cree. He was terribly embarrassed and wouldn't speak to Nellie for years. And he got his treaty status back as a result of our efforts. Nellie wasn't scared of anybody. A lot of our difficulties were within our own community, from our own people.

A Tribute to 71
Jenny Shirt Margetts

WHEN NELLIE AND KATHLEEN TELL THE STORY of Indian Rights for Indian Women, they return again and again to fond memories of their friend Jenny Margetts.

Jenny Marie Shirt Margetts was born on the Saddle Lake reserve on June 14, 1936, the daughter of Felix and Louisa Shirt, and a granddaughter of Angeline Batoche. She grew up in a family of ten children, and attended Blue Quill's Indian Residential School. At the age of sixteen, she began formal studies to become a nun. She left Alberta and spent the next five years at a convent in Beaupré, Quebec. There, she became fluent in French, her third language after Cree and English. While at the convent, she studied education, anthropology and sociology at Laval University in Quebec City. The young nun planned to become a teacher.

Returning to western Canada on a holiday, Jenny met her future husband Gordon Margetts, who owned a mobile welding business.

Having fallen in love with him, she began to reconsider her future. She decided to leave her religious vocation, marry and raise a family. After her marriage to Gordon in 1960, she lost her treaty rights and membership in the Saddle Lake Cree Nation.

The young couple moved to Saskatchewan, where Jenny attended a business college and began to work for a First Nations and Métis women's crafts co-operative. Returning to Edmonton with her husband and young family, she became more involved in the revitalized First Nations and Métis organizations of the mid-1960s. She was perfectly suited to this new wave of activism: assertive, articulate and determined.

She was a natural leader and innovator. For three years, she worked as an administrator for the new Alberta Native Communications Society, which produced radio programs broadcast across the province. She was fired from the position after she challenged the men who ran the organization on their business decisions, but she did not regret her departure. "It was then and there that I decided to fight, and grow," she would later tell an interviewer. "Actually it was during my time there that I discovered that native women were just going nowhere. They weren't taken seriously. They were expected to be at home. They were never expected to run for council, they were never expected to be political; we come from a very strong, chauvinistic society."

About 1970, Jenny joined the Voice of Alberta Native Women, a women's auxiliary group to the Indian Association of Alberta and the Métis Association of Alberta. In an interview, she remarked, "At the time I joined I thought, 'Hey! Alright! An organization for women! We're going to get someplace!'" She was subsequently disappointed with the limited focus of the group, but while working with them, she became interested in providing Cree language and cultural education for First Nations and Métis children. She led delegations to the legislature and wrote a brief for the Worth Commission on Native Education in Alberta. Jenny organized the Awasis program

Jenny Margetts.

with the first kindergarten set up at Prince Charles elementary school in Edmonton in 1973. She also travelled across northern Alberta, offering leadership training to women.

Like Nellie and Kathleen, who were both related to her through their Saddle Lake families, Jenny followed Jeannette Corbière Lavell's ongoing court case in the 1970s closely. At one Edmonton meeting with a representative of the federal Secretary of State's office, she began to talk about the sexual discrimination in the *Indian Act*. The rest is best told in Jenny's own words: "The young guy who was there, said to me: 'Have you ever thought of having a national conference? You have the skills to bring it together.' And I said, 'Where will I get the money?' and he said, 'From me. I'll help you if you're organizing behind the scenes.'" He arranged a $5,000 grant for the first national conference of First Nations and Métis women, which was held at the Hotel Macdonald.

For the rest of her life, Jenny served as the co-president of Indian Rights for Indian Women and as the spokesperson for the organization, along with Mary Two-Axe Earley. She and her husband Gordon raised three children, Tim, Kevin and Karen, and lived in Redwater, Alberta and in Edmonton. She died on October 18, 1991 after a three-year struggle with cancer.

Before she died, Jenny assembled a large collection of documents about First Nations and Métis political and social organizations, and comprehensive files on the work of the Indian Rights for Indian Women movement in Canada. In the summer of 2008, Gordon Margetts presented this collection to Dr. Brenda Macdougall, then of the Department of Native Studies at the University of Saskatchewan; Omeasoo Butt, a graduate student and research assistant at the university; and writer Linda Goyette so that the files could be indexed and preserved for the benefit of First Nations and Métis people and future researchers. Later, with agreement from Gordon Margetts and Dr. Macdougall, Nellie and Kathleen decided to donate the Jenny Margetts Collection to the Provincial Archives of Alberta.

◆ Nellie Carlson

Jenny's role in life was all about direction. She knew she wanted to finish school and have a vocation of her own. At that time, when she was young, going to the convent was often the only way.

When we moved to Edmonton, I never knew that Jenny had come back to Alberta from down east, or that she had married.

One day I was helping women to get ready for a meeting. It was in March 1967. I went to the Kingsway Hotel, downstairs, and I heard her talking as she was walking down the stairs. I saw Jenny. I saw a woman pointing to her, and saying: "Who is that?" And I said, "Don't you know? It's Jenny Shirt." She was with a white woman. At the coffee break, I got up and talked to her and said hello.

Jenny called me every morning for the next twenty-four years, right up until her death. She died October 18, 1991. That was the hardest part of my healing. Hearing the phone ring in the morning after she died—that would hurt me so much. I couldn't answer.

◆ Kathleen Steinhauer

Jenny was a classic worker. She could speak French, English and Cree. She had attended Catholic residential school, and was taken down east to Laval University in Quebec City to study early childhood education. She was planning on a life as a nun. In Quebec, she told us, she used to ring the bell to wake the other nuns in the convent. She saw a man crying in a dream. She phoned home to Saddle Lake. They said to her, "Come back. You do not belong there. We need you here." So she came back.

She later told us about her teachers, anthropologists and others. "They listened to us," she said. "We had white women as professors." Once Jenny made up her mind about something, she did it. She took university courses, and she liked research. That's probably why she was so careful with documents.

Jenny asked me to befriend the Papaschase people.[1] Descendants from Papastayo's band, like Maurice Quinn, had asked Jenny for help. This group was trying to get a reserve, and they were having a dreadful time. They had no resources, and we had no resources. We didn't have raffles or bingos or anything. In Indian Rights for Indian Women, we just concentrated on Section 12(1)(b). These people were searching for lawyers and a reserve in the late 1970s....

I looked at the old records of the people hatched, matched and dispatched. The old Cree names in the church records slowly became French names or English names, but they were the same people. Jenny realized that the treaty rights question, and the loss of treaty rights, was much larger issue than Section 12(1)(b)—these issues crossed over, and compounded one another.

NELLIE: In the early years in Edmonton Jenny was also involved with a parents' group. People from Driftpile reserve up north were living in the city, and they supported the idea of a Cree-language kindergarten. They were babysitting their grandkids, and they wanted them to speak Cree. The Awasis program was kindergarten and Grade One to begin with, and run by Jenny and a group of parents and a volunteer board.

The first kindergarten started with only seven kids. Co-op Cab provided transportation at first, but stopped because it had no insurance to carry kids regularly to school. We bought used vans, really cheap, for transportation for the kids. Jenny started negotiating with the Edmonton Public School Board for support. We sat up all night. Clive Linklater was helping us. He wrote two pages down of everything she had said. These ideas were taken to the school authorities and the system was changed. Awasis moved to Prince Charles School, which was full of native kids.

The parents were status and non-status Indians, working together on Indian education. I didn't realize it at the time that their co-operative work together would push ahead the Indian Rights for Indian Women cause. The parents didn't support Indian Rights for Indian Women but they didn't oppose us either. If we had done the same with a health care program, we could have brought even more people together.

Eventually [Alberta Education Minister] Dave King gave us provincial funding for the Awasis program. Many Cree and Métis people thought he helped out because his mother-in-law was Métis.

KATHLEEN: I said, "Jenny, you know the education bureaucracy is so thick you'll never get anywhere. She said, "Come here with me, we'll do it." And we did.

Mike Strembitsky was very good. He was the superintendent of education in Edmonton at that time. His family had been from around Smoky Lake, I think, not far from Saddle Lake. He was a progressive thinker, and he knew us. He supported the Awasis concept. And once it was set up, people came here from everywhere to see the program.

Jenny was always soliciting groups and individuals for money to keep the Awasis program going. She went to band councils all around Edmonton, and said, "You've got band members in the

city. Would you like the children to go to kindergarten in Cree?"
She persuaded Enoch band council to give her a cheque for
$1,000. The Alexander band gave them $1,000. Jenny received
$3,000 altogether. She wouldn't give it to the Native Friendship
Centre, which was supposed to keep the accounts. "We'll never
get it back," she said. She kept the cheque and used it for
transportation.

NELLIE: Once the school board adopted the program, it went up to
Grade Six. During her lifetime, Jenny didn't get the credit she
deserved for this innovation in Edmonton Public Schools. I nomi-
nated her as an Edmontonian of the Century in 2004 during the
city's centennial, but she should have been recognized when she
was alive.

Jenny wanted native liaison workers at every school, to work
with the families and keep our Cree students in school. Her work
with Awasis led to feasibility studies, and other kinds of education
studies of Cree language and cultural programs, in the Faculty of
Education and through School of Native Studies at the University
of Alberta, and this led to the founding of the Amiskwaciy
Academy—Canada's first urban Aboriginal high school.

Jenny said: "All doors should be opened to our students." In
the 1970s, there were only four university students who were
Aboriginal young people at the University of Alberta, two or three
status Indians and a Métis. Jenny said, "To be qualified to get
into university you need to get 70 per cent in Grade Twelve, and a
second language. All doors should be opened. A native language
should qualify as a second language, and should be taught in
elementary and high schools. Also the same education funding
should go to non-status Indians as status Indians for education. We need people in our communities with degrees: teachers,
nurses, social workers."

Many years later, Dr. Paul Davenport[2] saw me at the University
of Alberta education department. He was the president of the
university at that time. This was in the 1990s. He told me how

many First Nations students were enrolled, and how they could take any class they wanted. It took him that long to have all the doors opened at the University of Alberta. That long.

Every time a school bus goes to the front of my house, I think of Jenny. The Awasis program, she started it and it grew to 174 kids. That's the legacy she left all of us. She worked so hard as a leader with Indian Rights for Indian Women, too, even when she was ill. Even the medicine men said, "Take a break, Take a break." And she would say to me: "If I take a break, we will lose."

While assisting with the preparation of this book, Gordon Margetts found an audiotape of Jenny speaking to an unknown interviewer in the 1980s. On the tape, she describes the early days of Indian Rights for Indian Women and her own decision to become more outspoken about Indian Act discrimination. In 2007, Kendall Stavast, a student in the Faculty of Native Studies at the University of Alberta, donated many hours to the careful transcription of this partly inaudible tape. He also compiled a helpful file of newspaper coverage of Indian Rights for Indian Women in his work at the City of Edmonton Archives. The authors are grateful for his hard work. Here is an excerpt from the audiotape, as Jenny discusses her break with the Voice of Alberta Native Women organization over its reluctance to join the struggle against sexual discrimination in the Indian Act.

◆ Jenny Margetts

I asked that Section 12 of the *Indian Act* be discussed at a certain time in the morning [at the Voice of Alberta Native Women conference]. But during the night the president decided to call an emergency meeting with the executive. I was one of the executive members at the time and I wasn't called. They said they couldn't find me. And I said to them: "My husband was home. My kids were home."

So they pulled Section 12 of the *Indian Act* out of the agenda. There and then I decided it was futile [to expect more from Voice of

Alberta Native Women.] So I looked at the agenda and went to talk to the president, but she wouldn't even talk to me. Then she said: "Well, let's call on the full executive to find out what happened." I said "No. Don't even bother!"

So I went up to the podium at the conference, and I said: "The Voice of Native Women has achieved all of this in the past few years. We've done this and that, but the men want us to stick with the reserves. They don't want us to get politicized because then we would become a threat."

And I said, "Can't you understand that?" And these stoned-faced people looked at me.

I said: "We have an education, and we have trained all of these people. That's fine and dandy; that's great to do all of that. It's great to be working on education and foster care and all these services. But they [male leaders] want us to stick with services, you know, so we're no threat. Who travels to Ottawa? I never see any of your faces over there," I said. "It's always the men. I am writing cheques for men travelling to Ottawa with a Grade Three education and here I am with a university education and I can't go because I'm a woman. Does that sound fair? It isn't fair.

"We have to start working together," I said. "Right now we are just being muzzled by the Indian Association, the Métis Association, the Alberta Native Communications Society, you know, just male-dominated groups," I said. "None of you are sitting as board members; nobody is sitting as a chief, or sitting on band councils."

Then I thought about it. What do I do? I'm not going to stick around because I was just being killed. My own self-esteem was just going downhill like crazy. So they said that I had stolen some money, you know, some old garbage. One thousand, five hundred dollars went missing from some account. Then someone was saying that there was a resolution being passed around that I should never be in a position of authority anywhere. They did a real job on me. So this letter went to all native organizations and government departments.

At the time I felt sorry for myself. But I guess it didn't bother me that much because otherwise I would have had a nervous breakdown. What happened in the meantime, I was about three months pregnant, and I went to a conference in Saskatoon and this was a follow-up to the first National Native Women's Conference.

It would have been 1973. It had to be. Everything happened so fast in this period. So after the initial conference they had a panel about the pros and cons for the Lavell case. Right after that conference I did a talk at the podium. I said: "I quit the Voice of Alberta Native Women because it just won't do these things. It's a native women's rights organization, but it's not even trying to fulfill its mandate to work for native women's rights. You don't even know what women's rights are. You've got to learn. I'm willing to learn and I'm getting out, but you haven't heard the last of me."

kaskihowin/achievement

6

 How We Worked Together

THROUGH SMALL VICTORIES, significant defeats, and steady
disappointments, the activists of Indian Rights for Indian Women
kept working. By 1980 an estimated 15,000 women and 45,000 children had lost Indian status in Canada through the discriminatory
section of the *Indian Act*. Another 500 women were joining their
ranks every year, along with their children.

Indian Rights for Indian Women's long battle to change the law
dragged on for eighteen years, far longer than any of the women had
anticipated at the outset. They tried to encourage one another when
every court decision and parliamentary vote seemed to go against
them. They found new allies in unexpected places, but they endured
many challenges, too.

After working hard to obtain a small amount of funding for
their organizational efforts from the office of the federal Secretary
of State—which funded women's equality organizations across
Canada at the time—Ottawa cut off their grant pending a financial
audit. Several provincial women's organizations had complained

to the federal government about poor administration and financial mismanagement within Indian Rights for Indian Women, a claim Mary Two-Axe Earley and Jenny Margetts dismissed as "wild statements." The dispute involved a grant of $96,000, and was settled quickly, but it fractured the organization for a time. Activists from Alberta, Ontario and Quebec stayed together, and kept going. In this period, Jenny Margetts began her long struggle with cancer as she continued to lead the western wing of the organization. Nellie and Kathleen stood beside her throughout these ordeals.

The Indian Rights for Indian Women movement began an intensive lobby of Members of Parliament, cabinet ministers and senators in the mid-1970s. Determined to change the law, they were particularly frustrated because the Government of Canada could devote significant financial resources to defending the *Indian Act* in expensive court cases. In contrast, they had little money to support the court appeals of Jeannette Corbière Lavell and Yvonne Bédard or to organize an effective lobbying campaign. They depended on the generosity of family and friends, on law students and human rights lawyers who stood beside Indian Rights for Indian Women, and also on a few sympathetic outsiders who paid expenses from time to time. For women from the prairies, some with children and grandchildren at home, every lobbying trip to Ottawa presented huge challenges.

Back in Edmonton after these trips, Kathleen and Nellie always suspected RCMP surveillance. Sometimes it wasn't clear whether the surveillance and harassment of Indian Rights for Indian Women members came from opponents in First Nations treaty organizations, from angry individuals with treaty rights who feared the consequences of their activism, or from the RCMP. They would like future academic researchers to file a Freedom of Information request with the Government of Canada to determine whether they were followed, whether phone lines were tapped, or whether their mail was intercepted during their early activism. They contend that all of these incidents happened.

During the 1960s and 1970s, RCMP security services hired
informers within Aboriginal organizations and other political groups
they perceived as "extra-parliamentary opposition." The police covert
surveillance also included women's liberation groups, student
groups and certain university professors, peace groups, leftist and
labour groups. Canadian historians Steve Hewitt and Christabelle
Sethna have written extensively on RCMP infiltration of feminist
groups during the period. Nellie and Kathleen would like to know
whether Indian Rights for Indian Women was on the watch list.

As the 1980s began, the Government of Canada was preparing
to patriate the Constitution from Great Britain and to introduce a
new *Charter of Rights and Freedoms*. A new wave of public consultation, lobbying and court cases began. First Nations, Métis and Inuit
leaders argued that treaty and Aboriginal rights must be protected in
the new Constitution, and that patriation should not occur until their
outstanding grievances had been addressed. They claimed the right
to decide their own membership and the right to self-government
on reserves. Alberta and Saskatchewan chiefs travelled to London
in an attempt to block patriation in the British courts or Parliament
until treaty rights were guaranteed. Métis and non-status Aboriginal
leaders in the same provinces were eager for entrenched recognition in a new Constitution. Media coverage was heavy. Arguing about
their differences—and they differed on many topics—these leaders
began to educate the rest of the Canadian public about the diverse
aspirations of indigenous communities.

The activists of Indian Rights for Indian Women argued for
full equality and an end to *Indian Act* discrimination against them.
Sandra Lovelace,[1] a Maliseet woman from the Tobique Nation in New
Brunswick who had lost Indian treaty status after marriage, appealed
to the United Nations Human Rights Committee—a move that
embarrassed the government and brought international attention to
the women's cause.

At the constitutional talks in Ottawa, the Native Council of Canada
had two seats to represent Aboriginal people in Canada without

treaty status. Indian Rights for Indian Women formally requested a seat at the table. When the federal government refused the women's group, NCC president Harry Daniels gave up one of these seats to the women. Nellie and Kathleen remember the challenges of this period, but also their achievements.

◆ The Hard Work Begins

KATHLEEN: In the Indian Rights For Indian Women movement, we were very loyal to one another. We used to squabble, but we stuck together.

NELLIE: We had to work out a lot of issues. We were different ages, some in our thirties, some in our forties, some in our fifties. Philomena Ross and I were the older ones. We were so loyal to each other.

KATHLEEN: Even if we disagreed with one another, we would work it out. For example, Marie Marule went to work with the National Indian Brotherhood. George Manuel[2] was the president then, and the organization took a firm stand against our position.

NELLIE: Sometimes she was annoyed with us. I never talked to her about that. I remember an angry argument between Marie Marule and Jenny Margetts, when Jenny suggested that Marie was only interested in working for the NIB for money and not working with the women. Marie wouldn't take anything like that from anyone. She wouldn't take insults. Marie hit her hard. Jenny hit her right back. They got over this fight almost immediately. *[She laughs.]*

KATHLEEN: When the political parties had a political convention, I always thought some of our women from the Indian Rights for Indian Women should go and talk about Section 12(1)(b). Mary Two-Axe didn't want us to go, or indicate any political allegiance.

NELLIE: There was a Conservative meeting in Edmonton. Jenny Margetts was a Conservative.

KATHLEEN: I said to her, "If you're lobbying with us on this issue, you're not supporting the Conservatives, are you?" We had a disagreement on that. We both must have been in a bad mood.... We had to talk and talk to reach a consensus. Each woman had a strong personality. It wasn't easy. I remember a meeting in April 1978 at the Star of the North retreat house. We came up with fifteen resolutions and it was so difficult not to have it over-wordy. Women came from across Canada. I remember a woman named Rachel from Nova Scotia—not far from Halifax—and another woman, Martha. Rachel was heartbroken because her sons and grandson had married white women. According to the law, her great-grandchildren would not have Indian status. I remember other women from the Maritimes, for example Carol Warkman, her mother had lost status; she was a quiet woman but so knowledgeable. There were two older ladies from another reserve. We were Cree from Treaty Six area, but we worked with the Treaty Seven women and women from different backgrounds across Canada. At Sarcee, now Tsuu T'ina, if a woman married out, the couple and the kids had to leave the reserve, just like with us. Some women objected to this—Thelma King, Queenie Fox, Rufus Goodstriker's sister—and sometime Kainai women came to us from the Blood reserve.

NELLIE: Some women would come to us from the Treaty Seven area, and say: "You know, you are speaking on behalf of our daughters and our grandchildren."

KATHLEEN: We found it difficult to relate to the situation of the Inuit and Inuvialuit women in the Far North. The Inuit are all in one area, and they did not have treaties. We had to work with native women scattered all across Canada. The Inuit prefer these [land claims] agreements that they can negotiate and renegotiate. We had to work for legislation to change the *Indian Act*. It was different.

We had many friends on the outside, and they helped us a great deal. Marguerite Ritchie was a lawyer who helped us a lot.

Later some law students at the University of Alberta helped us so much, Jim Robb and Jean McBean...

NELLIE: These students were storefront lawyers many years ago at skid row on 96th Street.[3] There were seven of them. We got them interested. We told them what Section 12(1)(b) was all about. There were four of us who really knew about it: Philomena, myself and Kay and Jenny. Everything that we said, and everything that our grandfathers said, they wrote it down. They went to the university library and they looked it up, and we were right. They were so surprised. And so Jim Robb started writing papers for us. There were other ones. Davis. Beverly Brown. Jean McBean... Already they knew it was a very dicey issue.

William Harris, the historian, was really good, too, but he left town. There were many others who supported our cause.

KATHLEEN: We took our case to local Members of Parliament. An Edmonton MP Steve Paproski got us a meeting with Jean Chrétien, who was Minister of Indian Affairs at that time. And at an early meeting at the Edmonton Friendship Centre, we invited Paul Yewchuk, a Conservative MP from Alberta.

NELLIE: The first time he met us he was so hard on us. He kept asking, "Why?" We said: "Why are you so hard on us?" He said: "Because those are the kind of questions you are going to receive from those who oppose you."

✦ Taking the Fight to Ottawa

KATHLEEN: Jeannette Corbière Lavell's case in the Supreme Court of Canada gave us the spark. We had always talked, but no one had done anything.

NELLIE: I was going to travel on the train to Ottawa [when the case was heard]....We went with elders, three old ladies named Hermine Anderson, Veronica Morin, and Philomena Ross's mother...

A young Indian girl got on the train in Sioux Lookout. She was very sick, and sitting with an older woman. We were near her,

Philomena Aulotte, Nellie Carlson and Jenny Margetts in Gibbons, Alberta.
[Photo by Pamela Harris]

sitting with two University of Saskatchewan students, two men, on our way to Ottawa. We were telling them about the Lavell case.

Veronica Morin and some others were sitting near the girl, and I heard them saying in Cree: "He should leave that girl alone because she is sick." Another man was there. He was talking rough to the older ladies and trying to get the girl to go to the bar. I went over there. I said: "Sir you know you don't belong here. Why don't you leave that girl alone and go sit where you belong?" Then he tells me to mind my own business. He calls me "a damn Indian woman." He said something about being an expert in karate. I tapped him on his shoulder, and then I pushed him down. "You sit where you belong," I said, "or I'll put you in an

Indian death hold." *[She starts to laugh.]* I didn't even know what an Indian death hold was! Philomena Ross woke up and laughed so loud! Oh, that man was mad at us! I was so scared of him but I never even showed it. I said, "I'm sorry. We couldn't sleep because you wouldn't leave her alone." He jumped off at the next stop. The young boys told me he had a gun and he had a knife. He was a drug dealer. The next morning in Armstrong, Ontario he got off the train.

KATHLEEN: And when she got home from Ottawa, she called me to tell me this story, and she was laughing and saying, "I don't even know what an Indian death hold is. I made it up." And I said: "You were lucky!"

NELLIE: *[Laughing.]* I think I heard about an Indian death hold in the movies....We had lots of fun. When we arrived in Ottawa, we had a room in the Chateau Laurier hotel....Suddenly we saw a snake under the door. It smelled like sweetgrass. We knew what it meant. We were so glad. The phone began to ring. I decided to smudge that phone and I did. Finally the [harassment] calls just quit coming.

The next day the Lavell case was to be heard in the Supreme Court of Canada. Many chiefs had come to Ottawa to oppose the women's court case, including Chief John Snow from Alberta. At 10 A.M., Margaret Hyndman, the lawyer who helped Indian Rights for Indian Women, asked the RCMP to take us upstairs, to escort us. He told us to go upstairs to take our seats. He opened the door for eight of us, and more came later. There were two from Nova Scotia, and some from Ontario. We forgot to tell Mary Two-Axe Earley. She went through the crowd alone. There was a lot of name calling and swearing at her. It was terrible for her. We went all the way to Ottawa to hear that case, and we lost.

I was told the chiefs would have a meeting with the Department of Indian Affairs. Someone said: "Nellie, would the elders be willing to go and listen? Please try and tell them to go and listen." Then I said, "Okay, we will." It was as windy as could be, but they went. Eight old ladies went there to listen to the meeting. The men were saying: "Oh I get it. Nellie delegates these women to go to the National Indian Brotherhood meeting to listen to us." That told me they're not doing the right thing. They're going against the women.

When she came back, Veronica Morin told us: "Some men got up and gave us space to sit down. There are leaders there, half asleep. Harold Cardinal and George Manuel are talking about suggested revisions to the *Indian Act*." And she heard that the government people flew Indian leaders to see a hockey game in Montreal. We heard it on Monday morning.

KATHLEEN: We were used to that sort of thing. That's how the government behaved with Indian people. There was a demonstration in Edmonton after Jeannette Corbière Lavell lost her case. My son Gilbert Jr. came, he was only four and a half at the time. We all wore black.

NELLIE: Later on we decided to make a presentation to the Standing Committee on Indian Affairs. They ran out of time on their agenda, and it looked like they would have no time for us. I said to them: "We are well prepared to sit with you all night." We sat with them until midnight. We waited for many hours with nothing to eat or drink. I was there with Pauline Harper, Jenny Margetts's sister from Toronto. We made the points, really good points.

We were asked about the rights of the Métis. I said, "I think we have to recognize they did not want to live under the tyranny of the government either." Harry Daniels was pleased I said that.

KATHLEEN: When Bill C-31 was finally passed, the Métis realized the big boat Tyranny was turning around for them too.

NELLIE: We used to have a roomful of opposition people. A war bride, surname Ahenakew, was there, and talked to Harold Cardinal. She wanted to speak. Stan Daniels wanted to speak, but only the women, the Indian Rights for Indian Women delegates, were allowed to speak that time. The MPS would meet with us—a dozen or fifteen of us at the most. The elders insisted to us that

Jenny say at the end of her presentation: "The Queen of England should apologize." Jenny said it with a perfectly straight face.

KATHLEEN: Nellie wanted us to meet the national Indian leaders. One of the women told us: "It is not the men who want this law. It is this building." She meant the Department of Indian Affairs and the Government of Canada.

NELLIE: When we were visiting MPS, we always said: We are going to sue the government because it was their fault that this was happening to us. Mary Two-Axe Earley would tell them, "Five hundred cats and dogs on the Kahnawake reserve have more rights than we do, or our children do. We are rapidly losing our language and culture."

KATHLEEN: Mary was a very good negotiator. She had a very solid and reasonable answer for every question. She was very firm and determined, but she wasn't abrasive.

NELLIE: Often we said things that were insulting, and they were insulting when I think about them. Different people had different ways of negotiating.

KATHLEEN: Some negotiators were upfront and combative. Jenny Margetts was reasonable and constructive, and she could make · a point after Nellie got their attention! *[She laughs.]* If you want people to support you, you have to show some respect for them. Sometimes I'd get so upset with Nellie because she would make so many enemies....Sometimes Nellie said things that shocked people to the core. When she was talking about women who gained treaty status by marrying band members, she would say: "They must be Indian by injection."

NELLIE: Politicians often liked to mention that they had Aboriginal ancestry, as if that meant a certain kinship even if they did nothing to end *Indian Act* discrimination. So Jean Chrétien said to Jenny in a meeting, "You know, I have to tell you that I'm one of you." And Jenny said: "That's totally irrelevant to us." We weren't getting anywhere. The government kept promising legislation, every season, but it didn't happen.

KATHLEEN: When we got closer to the time when the Constitution was patriated, between 1980 and 1982, we were given more funding to do our work. But earlier on, it was very tough. None of us had any money. On one early trip to Ottawa, someone gave us two $5 bills. We saved that for our meals only. Jenny would go to a store and buy fruit, bread and tea bags.

NELLIE: When Iona Campagnolo was the Minister Responsible for the Status of Women, I met her assistants in Ottawa. I said I am using my own money going around in cabs. I was from Edmonton....I've got more children at home. I am living with Section 12(1)(b) and my children are too. She helped us get money for taxi fare and lunches. Jenny didn't want to spend the money.... Maybe they thought we'd take their money and shut up. Later I said to Hugh Faulkner, who was Secretary of State: "Your highly paid workers go against us while this case is in the Supreme Court." It wasn't fair.

The National Indian Brotherhood and other groups were so opposed to us. We had this one meeting with cabinet ministers. Mr. Trudeau didn't come, of course, but Marc Lalonde[4] was there. They were introducing themselves to us. They wanted to say they had discussed the issue with us but we didn't really feel that they listened to us. On the way home, we were so exhausted. Yet could still find silly jokes to cheer one another up. For example, once Jenny was eating and a kernel of corn fell on her lap. She said, "I've got a colonel between my legs." You have to laugh because it hurts too much to cry...

This one issue of treaty rights and Aboriginal rights across Canada was tightly controlled by the government, so that it would never be talked about across the country. The white people were scared that the opposition would spread. Mary Two-Axe Earley told us there was a lot of support from the Quebec media, but over here, in western Canada, no.

KATHLEEN: In those days, we resented the amount of money that Native Women's Association of Canada received for workshops, meetings and conferences when we didn't receive it. Iona Campagnolo helped to register the national Indian Rights for Indian Women committee, but the funding disparities continued.

After these meetings in Ottawa, opponents and supporters would call us. A lot of these women used to phone me and try to get the information out of me. And I would say: "All I am is a transporter and a breadwinner. I don't tell you more than that." But the calls were really heavy through day and night.

◆ Surveillance and Harassment

NELLIE: These were hard times for us. Our lives were threatened, our phones were tapped, our mail was confiscated and opened. I said to Elmer once that I was going to ask Trudeau to at least assign a young and handsome man to follow us! I also told Elmer I wanted a camera to take a picture of the old man following us. I thought he must be a retired RCMP officer.

KATHLEEN: We would hear the clicks and bangs on the telephone. Someone told us, "It's just the RCMP changing the tape." I wouldn't believe them for the longest time, but then I read about similar surveillance in the United States, and the clicking sound. We knew our phones were tapped. You'd hear this noise when you were answering the phone. I talked to someone about clicks on the line, and changes in the sound of the call. Both sounds were unfamiliar to me in a regular phone call. And he said, "That's nothing. They are just changing the tape."

NELLIE: We always suspected RCMP surveillance. It was going on at that time with a lot of the Indian organizations.

KATHLEEN: We knew people who had been approached by the RCMP to spy on other organizations and report what was happening. There was a lot of talk at the time about AIM, the American Indian Movement, and radicals. RCMP officers were approaching people and asking them to inform on one another.

NELLIE: Throughout this time, we were also harassed by opponents—strangers who wouldn't give their name. Jenny phoned me one night after 10:30 and mentioned to me that she had received a call. The voice had said: "Watch yourself." It was a threatening call. The caller was saying something about blowing our heads off, one by one. Jenny said to the caller: "If you are man enough to do this, why won't you say who you are?" I had received some of these calls, too. She was feeling very upset. She said: "I don't know why we are receiving these calls." I said: "Don't worry. We are now swimming in that river called negativity." I said, "Sometime we will reach the other shore and we will find the positive energy waiting for us."

One night in Ottawa, we were outside the Standing Committee of Indian Affairs at midnight after an evening meeting. A man came to us and said: "Jenny Margetts, I'm going to shoot you." This man was later deported. They were so mean to us. That is why we were so mean in return.

Indian Rights for Indian Women had an office in Edmonton at 130 Street, off the St. Albert Trail, in a welding business, Ranger Trailer Repair. Jenny had done some bookkeeping for the business, and they rented space to us. We were always worried about break-ins. Women volunteered to stay there at night. We had smashed-up vans, sometimes. These vans belonged to the Awasis program and they were for picking up kids and taking them to school. They belonged to the Friendship Centre. These vans had their windows smashed in, and we knew who did it. Gordon [Margetts] gave a pack of beer to bikers to scare those guys. The bikers chased those guys all the way to BC! [She laughs.]

◆ The Patriation of the Constitution

KATHLEEN: The men who led the Indian Association of Alberta and the National Indian Brotherhood were against the patriation of the Constitution before 1982, and they led a huge campaign against it. They were afraid of the loss of treaty rights. Indian Rights for Indian Women welcomed patriation. We understood that if the Constitution came home to Canada, the *Charter of Rights and Freedoms* would supersede the *Indian Act.*

NELLIE: Harry Daniels of the Native Council of Canada was listening to us. He made a place for us at the table. It worked that way during the lobbying before the patriation of the Constitution. When we didn't have the right accreditation, different women would give us theirs so we could get into these meetings. A man from Meadow Lake couldn't come. He gave his daughter his nametag so she could go. She gave it to me. At that time, in the room, were Ovide Mercredi,[5] Willie Littlechild,[6] Mike Mitchell, Eddie Head. All the men stood there. I said, "I'm here on behalf of Jenny Margetts, president of Indian Rights for Indian Women." I talked about the opposition we had. I said we hope all the descendants are guaranteed their rights. I'm talking about the Métis people too. I spoke in Cree.

I sat there. I knew we were hated. I knew deep down that people resented us. You are not there for yourself. You are there for the people who are affected by the law.

Before talking to the Standing Committee on Indian Affairs, I fasted for twenty-four hours before, no food, no water, for spiritual strength. They said they had already had a delegation of native women.

Jenny said: "We are well prepared to sit with you all night. We came here all the way from Edmonton, Alberta to speak to you." We only outlined the main points.

Well, then, after that, we were notified by phone in Edmonton that airline tickets were waiting for us to come to Ottawa for a special meeting. Mary Two-Axe Earley would be there, too. We were going to meet cabinet ministers and the prime minister, Mr. Trudeau, to talk about this issue.

♦ Meeting Pierre Trudeau

We went to meet Trudeau. They took us through the west block of the Parliament Buildings and underground. This lady had a card, a door opened and we went through. The next door opened. There was a big round table in a cabinet room. All the cabinet was there but two or three. I remember Francis Fox and Marc Lalonde were there.

Philomena Ross said, "We are the dispossessed." We explained that we were still on the General List of treaty Indians not necessarily attached to bands. We said, "They never took us off the General List." Philomena said her father on his deathbed told her to fight for her son's right to be on the reserve. Her son had lost his oil royalties due to the marriage of his mother. The rules had been put in the *Indian Act* in 1956, and the son had been born in 1955. It took her eleven years to get him reinstated for his royalties. And 407 people were reinstated across Canada who had lost rights after that 1956 ruling.

Trudeau said to us: "Why don't you take up this problem with the chiefs, with the National Indian Brotherhood leadership, and they will listen to you." And I said to him right away: "Bullshit, they will!" And Mary Two-Axe Earley kicked me hard under the table for swearing. I could hardly walk out of there.

Yes, he told us to go and talk to the National Indian Brotherhood. "You should go and see your chiefs," he said. "That's when I said that, and Mary Two-Axe Earley kicked me under the table. I tried to tell him: "They don't look at us. We don't exist to them." Mary Two-Axe would say: "Their pets can be buried on their own reserve in pet cemeteries. But we can't be buried on our reserve." Marc Lalonde sat with his feet on the windowsill. He wasn't taking us seriously. We were so determined to make changes.

Whenever they asked, "Do you want to move back to the reserve," I said, "I don't know. I would like to have the choice like my brothers, my father and all the men."

Trudeau said, "I guess it's time we brought the Constitution home."[7]

◆ Discrimination within the *Indian Act*

NELLIE: Bill C-47 was a Liberal Bill, a first try. Indian women and children would be brought into treaty, but grandchildren would be negotiable. It went through the House of Commons to the Senate. Charlie Watt,[8] the Inuit senator, voted against it, and the Bill died. That time we cried.

Later I went to see him in his Ottawa office. Me and Clarice went to see him. I said, "You damn so-and-so. You must be married to a white woman." I said to him, "You only thought about yourself, not your mother, your sister, your daughters, only you." You could see tears coming into his eyes. And I said to him: "We don't want to hear you say, 'Sorry.' We don't. What words would be coming from your mother?"

We almost won our case when the Liberals introduced Bill C-47. We lost that one. I never cry, but that time I cried."

KATHLEEN: We got to this point. We had made all of our submissions, lobbied the government, went to meetings with everyone, and we were still waiting.

7

 Fighting for Our Birthright

NELLIE AND KATHLEEN FELT AS IF THEY HAD WAITED for an eternity, but finally the day came. On June 28, 1985, the Parliament of Canada passed Bill C-31 to bring the *Indian Act* into line with the equality guarantees in the *Charter of Rights and Freedoms*, which had come into effect on April 17th. They had finally defeated the loathed Section 12(1)(b).

The federal government promised that the new amendments would remove sexual discrimination from the *Indian Act* and restore Indian status and membership rights for all women who had been disinherited since 1951, as well as for two generations of their children. In the legislation, the federal government maintained control over who would be registered as an Indian and the rights that would flow from membership on a General List. The First Nations gained new legal authority to decide who could live on a reserve, and to create membership codes.

It was a significant victory for the women, but not a complete one. Some First Nations refused to offer full rights and benefits to the reinstated members, claiming that they had no resources and not enough land to accommodate more families. Several wealthy Alberta First Nations with significant oil and gas resources—Sawridge, Ermineskin and Tsuu T'ina—went to court to challenge Bill-31 promises to the reinstated members.

The most controversial part of the Bill C-31 amendment remains the so-called "second-generation cut-off." Under the new regulations, Indian status can be terminated after two successive generations of intermarriage between Indians and non-Indians. In the future, a child would have to have at least two status Indian grandparents to claim Indian status. Not long after they saw Bill C-31 in practice, women realized that the old gender discrimination had crept back into the *Indian Act* by a side door.

Sharon McIvor, an Indigenous activist, legal scholar and academic, and a member of the Lower Nicola Indian band, reclaimed her status through Bill C-31 but recognized that some of her grandchildren would be penalized unfairly. She began a court challenge in 1989. Her case successfully argued that Bill C-31 rules still gave preferential treatment to people who trace their First Nations heritage paternally through their father's family rather than maternally through their mother's family. The British Columbia Court of Appeal agreed on this point, saying that the new rules infringed on equality rights. To conform to the ruling, the federal government amended the *Indian Act* again in late 2010 to remove some aspects of gender discrimination. From now on, eligible grandchildren of women who lost status after marriage will be entitled to Indian status.[1] As a result of McIvor's legal challenge, another 45,000 people became eligible for registration.

However, McIvor remains concerned that the *Indian Act* continues to allow gender discrimination against many Aboriginal women and their descendants. Specifically, she says the law still excludes descendants of registered Indian women who co-parented with non-status men in common law unions; grandchildren of disinherited Indian women born before 1951, and the illegitimate female children of male Indians. "Bill C-31 will not even confer equal registration status on those who will be newly eligible," she wrote in a letter to Members of Parliament in November 2010. "The 'second-generation cut-off' will apply to the female line descendants a generation earlier than it does to their male line counterparts."

McIvor told the MPS she was preparing to file a complaint against Canada at the United Nations Human Rights Committee in Geneva. "My own struggle has taken twenty years," she said in her letter. "Before me, Mary Two-Axe Earley, Jeannette Corbière Lavell, Yvonne Bédard and Sandra Lovelace all fought to end discrimination against Aboriginal women in the status registration provisions in the *Indian Act*. It has been about fifty years now. Surely this is long enough."

The Government of Canada filed its response to McIvor's complaint with the United Nations in September 2011. At the time of this book's publication, McIvor and her supporters are waiting for a ruling.

Nellie and Kathleen followed the McIvor case with interest. They, too, feel the rules are not yet fair. Still they have found good reasons to celebrate as thousands of disinherited First Nations—including their own husbands and children—applied for Indian status, and retrieved a status or treaty card and some limited benefits. Since Bill C-31 has passed, the number of registered Indians in Canada has more than doubled, from about 360,000 in 1985 to 824,341 in 2010.

Their own fierce struggles with the *Indian Act* continued after the passage of Bill C-31. Like McIvor, they had unfinished business with the Government of Canada.

In July 1992, Kathleen Steinhauer began a long legal battle to be reinstated as a full member of the Saddle Lake Cree Nation. She was not content to be returned to the Kainai Nation list as she had lived on the Blood reserve for just a few years during her first marriage. Nor did she want her name on the General List of registered Indians, that long list kept by the Department of Indian Affairs as a catch-all for individuals who were not attached to a particular First Nation. That's where many reinstated families had been listed, partly because some of their communities of origin had instituted new membership codes to try and exclude them. The idea didn't sit right with Kathleen. It didn't satisfy her sense of fairness. She wanted her full name—Kathleen Amelia Jane Steinhauer—restored to the Band List of her own Cree nation, her birthplace. She emphasizes that her quarrel was with the Government of Canada, not with the people of Saddle Lake. "They didn't write the *Indian Act*," she said. "The Government of Canada was responsible for what happened to us."

Her campaign took seven years, but she succeeded. She says it was a point of principle.

◆ Kathleen Steinhauer

When Bill c-31 was passed, I had every expectation that I would be returned to the Saddle Lake Band List. In fact, I filled out my application to that effect. I hadn't lived on the Blood reserve for more than twenty years, and my time there was brief. I'd only lived at the Blood reserve as an employee of the hospital, and at the time of my first marriage to Allan Small Face. I had two good friends from the Blood tribe in Pauline Gladstone and Georgina Davis, but that was the extent of my ties. When my marriage dissolved, I went straight back to Saddle Lake. That was my home!

Anyway, I was really horrified to receive a letter saying that I would be returned to the Blood Band List.

Right after Bill c-31 was passed in Ottawa, we had a meeting at Jenny's house at Redwater on a long weekend. Other Indian Rights for Indian Women members were there. This was in early July. The Bill had been passed in late June and there were quite a few of the women there. We asked Jim Robb to come, and he sent Anne McLellan.[2] She was sure cold and dry, but when she got elected it was something different.

We were going through this Bill together. It was very difficult legal language. Anne's job was to explain this legislation to us. They came to one clause, and I didn't understand it. Nellie turned to me and she

Kathleen Steinhauer appealed to the Federal Court of Canada in 1992 to restore her Saddle Lake Cree membership status. She won the case in 1999.

said, "This is going to apply to you, Kay. You're going to be returned to the Blood Band List, not Saddle Lake."

She was right about that. I asked Doug Stephansson of Indian Affairs later about it. He explained that a lot of women with treaty rights had married into another band, to a man with treaty rights. The federal government didn't want the administrative inconvenience of transferring all of these women back to their original Band Lists, to the reserve where they had been born. So they left it to say that those of us who had lost our status through marriage would get it back to the band where we had been enfranchised.

As a result of this I was left to figure out a solution. We always asked Jim Robb questions when we ran up against a brick wall. He suggested that I write a letter asking the Saddle Lake leadership for a band council resolution restoring my membership there. I did that, but they didn't answer at all. Then I sent a memo to Steve Paproski, our Member of Parliament at the time, and asked him to help me resolve this. I also had a meeting with Don Mazankowski in Vegreville.[3] He said, "Good God" when I showed him the documents. I don't think politicians had any idea what we were up against. Mazankowski was minister of practically everything, as well as deputy prime minister at one time. His wife and I had been in nursing training together. Eventually I received a letter from the Department of Indian Affairs saying they would look into it.

Some Edmonton lawyers did some research for Indian Rights for Indian Women on this matter with a $1,300 little grant we received from the Secretary of State. In the end, they said there was nothing we could do about it. And I said, enough of *that* nonsense.

I finally went to Jean McBean. She had worked with the Indian Rights for Indian Women with Jim Robb when she was a law student, right from the very beginning. She did a lot of research. She said, okay, we will have to launch a *Charter* challenge. She told me she needed $500 to do this, and do you know, she gave it back as soon as we won the case. I phoned her every two or three weeks for an update. She used to say, "If it were anyone else I'd drop the case right now." It was very difficult for all of us. This went on for years and years.

One day she phoned me and said, "I want you to come to my office and meet someone who is prepared to help us." That's the first time I met Dr. Dale Gibson.[4] He'd come out here to Alberta for love, and then stayed after he got married. He was a very humble man but very knowledgeable about the *Charter*. After a time, he left one law firm for another, but he told me, "I'll continue to work with Jean on this issue of yours on my own time."

Dale was excellent. If you met him, you'd never know he was a
PHD in law. He had written legal textbooks. Jean and Dale were both
active in the early years of LEAF, the organization that raised money
for women's *Charter* challenges. Jean was on the board, and Dale
was one of the first men on the board. Dale and Jean got right down
to work on this. Jean would let me know about court management
meetings. Dale had contributions to make from his experience. As
Dale called it, we started to make glacial progress.

At one point we were told that we had to delay our own case until
Walter Twinn's case[5] had proceeded through the courts. This was
very slow because at one point the courts told Twinn's lawyers to
return with a better case.

At the same time, this gave Dale more time to do in-depth prep-
arations. We had hoped to hire two or three Aboriginal lawyers or
legal researchers to work beside them on this case. We asked two or
three Aboriginal lawyers, and they said no. I don't blame them. People
on reserves had been raised with this very painful issue in their own
families. They all thought there was no way to change the law. They
tended to forget that the *Indian Act*'s rules on women's membership
rights had been changed many times before. Why was the government able to change the membership rules with such ease? What
was the government policy behind the red ticket? I want these questions in the book. I hope this research will be done some day.

Women who had qualified for this "red ticket" retrieved their treaty
status right away after the passage of Bill c-31. One of our members,
Mary Louise Frying Pan of Frog Lake, had this experience. As for me,
my case went on and on. I waited. The first letter that I still have
from Jean McBean on my legal case is dated 1990, and I believe I
went to her in 1987. We didn't win until 1999, but I had complete
faith in both Jean and Dale all the way. I knew they were excellent
lawyers, top in their profession. I knew Jean would never take no
for an answer.

We finally got court dates, probably in 1997 or 1998. We had asked Mary Louise Frying Pan and her husband Dolphus Frying Pan to be expert witnesses, also Philomena Aulotte who lived on her own farm at Fishing Lake Métis settlement. Philomena and her husband Robert Aulotte had homesteaded before the settlement came into existence, and they had raised many foster children.

They were constant members of Indian Rights for Indian Women, Mary Louise and Philomena. Nellie was along with me the whole time, and she offered to be a witness and also a Cree translator.

One fine summer day we drove out to Fishing Lake with Dale Gibson. We met with Dolphus and Mary Louise at an elders' lodge where Philomena was waiting for us. Dale asked us questions. Nellie and Philomena translated for Mary Louise. She could speak English but she preferred to speak Cree. She and Dolphus said it was tradition that when a Cree couple married, the husband moved to live with the woman's family. Hugh Dempsey and Tony Fisher had written this too. I knew this in my mind but I didn't relate it to the legal question. You see, men had moved from Frog Lake to Saddle Lake after marriage, and they had been accepted as band members. That was key. The elders knew that. For example Alice Steinhauer had married a Quinney from Frog Lake, and he came to live in Saddle Lake.

Dale and Nellie and I talked to these elders, and they explained Cree marriage custom and traditions. Driving back from Fishing Lake, Nellie fell asleep in the car and Dale and I began to talk about the residential school question. We had been hearing about lawyers contacting people about possible lawsuits. I said, "Could you find out what's really happening for us?" He said, yes, he would. People had been getting phone calls from law firms. He arranged a meeting and said to be sure to bring Gilbert along because his input would be helpful. Gilbert hadn't been to residential school but he was chief of the Michel Band then. Five or six Indian Rights for Indian Women members joined us. Before we knew it, we were pursuing a case on residential school issues. We hadn't finished this one court case and here we were up to our necks in another one!

The lawyers for Saddle Lake said they needed six weeks of court time, and they'd have one hundred elders to testify—some exorbitant number like that. We finally had a trial date. The room was set up in a hotel downtown, with a security guard. We saw elders there from Saddle Lake and Goodfish Lake, including Edith Memnook, who had been Edith Jackson and a relative of Nellie's, and Elmer Redcrow. Several of the people from Saddle Lake gave me dirty looks, scowling at me. But one former chief and band councillor related to me came and talked to us. They acknowledged this was a pretty difficult situation for all of us.

As I look back I think this situation was not really the fault of the leadership at Saddle Lake. The *Indian Act* was the federal government's way to confuse the First Nations in a certain way to cover up for the land that had been stolen. It led to an atmosphere of fear that the reinstated women would spread their influence to the community. I always thought the opposition was all about fear, and the federal government was to blame.

The lawyers had warned us that if this case didn't go our way we might owe a lot of money, and some supporters thought they might lose their house and all. So Nellie and I were on our own again. Other friends were far away but I knew they were with me.

Court Hearing: Federal Court of Canada, Edmonton

On the day of the hearing I was asked to testify. The lawyers for Saddle Lake asked me a series of questions. Why I wanted to go to Saddle Lake, why I wanted to belong to the Saddle Lake band. I gave my reasons in my testimony. The lawyer questioned whether the judge had jurisdiction in this matter, and I don't think the judge liked that much. That was Judge Douglas Campbell.

I was nervous because Saddle Lake had been threatening to bring so many elders to testify against me. We ended up chatting with our relatives in the lobby beforehand. Gilbert happened to be sitting

beside two elders, speaking in Cree, and he heard one say: "You know we put this medicine on her, and it didn't work." They didn't know my husband understood Cree.

Many elders from Saddle Lake were there. The lawyers for Saddle Lake called Henry Quinney as their expert witness. In the courtroom we had a conversation, and he asked me: "How are we related again?" and I told him. Henry's mother, Edna, and my father, Ralph Steinhauer, were first cousins. Henry's grandparents were Augustine and Charlotte Steinhauer; Charlotte was sister to Josiah Apow, who was my father's father, who died when he was three or four.

When Henry Quinney testified, he said Saddle Lake band only wanted members who believed in peace, order and good government. The lawyer asked whether Kathleen Steinhauer presented a problem in that regard. He said no. The lawyer asked whether Saddle Lake band council ever accepted new members. He said, yes, by band council resolution. Would the band accept returning members due to the passage of Bill c-31? He said no.

Jean told the court: "This is not about money."[6]

Outside the hearing Edith Memnook—she was related to Peter Lougheed[7] through the Hardisty family—said to me: "We can't afford the welfare bill for all of these people coming in." I said, "Edith, it's not about money or welfare. We are working people, and don't want the money. It is the principle." These hearings in July led to a final session, with the judgement. On that last day, nobody from Saddle Lake was there. They knew they'd failed in their arguments. The judge ruled in our favour. I was relieved. I didn't see how anybody who believes in the *Charter of Rights and Freedoms* could turn us down.

Nellie had given me a beaded pendant to wear, a prayer wheel like an eight-point star. When traditional Cree people pray, they pray for these gifts such as wisdom, courage, protection as represented by the points on the prayer wheel. She said, "Wear this at the trial." When

< *Top: Gilbert and Kathleen often performed together, and shared a passion for the preservation of traditional Métis music and dancing. Gilbert was well known across the prairies as a fiddler, and in his final years taught young students to play the authentic tunes of their heritage. Bottom: After a long, happy and productive life, Kathleen Steinhauer died on March 4, 2012.*

I was finished I gave it back to her. Other women in our group had also worn it when they needed it.

After the judge ruled in my favour, we went out with Dale to his cabin for a meeting. Jean and Dale were ecstatic. Jean said we succeeded in all seven points we put forward. Oh, they were two fine people! They asked for another hearing to get a court order for my reinstatement as a Saddle Lake Cree member, so that the Acting Registrar would transfer my name to the Saddle Lake Band List.

At the time the Blood band had its own membership code, but Saddle Lake did not because the council could not get enough votes to support it.[8]

I had been so afraid of testimony from Joe P. Cardinal[9] and his wife as they were the most respected elders in Saddle Lake. But, at one time, Joe P. met me and said, "The woman is the heart of the home," and I sensed he understood me. We were all close relatives. That makes sense to me.

I always thought I should have a get-together with Jean and her husband John, and Dale and Sandra, to celebrate our case. Dale was a down-to-earth person but when he talked to a judge he was all-lawyer. Magnificent! I get tears in my eyes when I think of everything Jean and Dale did for me.

I have asked my children and grandchildren to go on the Saddle Lake list too if they want. But they want to join the Michel band through their father because of where we live. After Bill C-31 passed, Gilbert's name went on the General List. One time we were going down to the United States, to a fiddle competition, and at the border we were asked for two pieces of identification. We both showed our driver's licence and our treaty cards. That felt good. Our whole raison d'être was restoring treaty rights for our children.

8

 **This Is Our Land**

THE FAMILY IS THE HEARTBEAT OF CREE CULTURE. Elders are
the true teachers. Nellie and Kathleen describe their struggle to
protect treaty and Aboriginal rights as a personal obligation to their
families, to their descendants, and to all people of the First Nations.
But they have more to say about the recovery and preservation of
rich traditions, the celebration of identity. They want to help a new
generation escape the destructive mentality that the *Indian Act* and
centuries of European paternalism imposed on Aboriginal people. In
this chapter, Nellie Carlson speaks directly to young people, asking
them to break free.

◆ Nellie Carlson

Under the clan system, all people were recognized, and belonged.
We were absolutely brainwashed by the *Indian Act*. In the old days,
before Alberta became a province, the Cree leader Bobtail, Kiskayo,

had eight daughters. Every daughter married someone from a different reserve.

My mother told me before her death about the women's clan system in the Saddle Lake area. Men had their own tasks. A lot of women knew about the traditional ways. They hunted, snaring and hunting rabbits and other animals. They made their own gardens together. Women got along. Sometimes if a band didn't have enough members of one gender, they would bring in new members from another reserve. For example, at one time, Saddle Lake did not have enough women. They brought in Stoney and Sarcee members, and sometimes families adopted people from other reserves. Only eleven families are original to Saddle Lake.

Whether you have treaty status according to the law or not, you're still a Cree person if you have that family lineage. Right from the beginning I've always felt that.

My daughter, my oldest girl, went to school in a white school. And she said to me: "We cannot find anything about the Indian people to learn." She asked me, can I go and speak to the students? She was in Grade Four. All we could find then were two sentences, or one paragraph, or something like that, four lines, about Indian people. I went to my mother-in-law. I asked her to give me some hide, moccasins, and I took some along to the school. She gave me dried meat, dried fish and berries. I talked about tipis. The kids were really surprised in Grades Four, Five and Six. It was the same here in Edmonton when I talked in O'Leary High School in social studies.[1]

When they first opened Amiskwaciy Academy,[2] I wasn't there. One day I decided to go and see it. I went by cab. When I got there I smiled. These kids had their own school. They asked me later if I would serve as an elder at the school. In my mind, it never occurred to me to call myself an elder. Someone has to know their culture, has to know their language. You have to be a role model. And I'm not a role model. I'm the most horrible person, once considered public enemy number one by some people. I went home to tell my husband.

I went back the next day. I told them, "I've come to feel my way around." They said I have to sit at the meetings whenever the students are suspended. I agreed. I was asked to go to the classroom. I like to see who is focused to come and learn. I talk to them about the *Indian Act*, the history of Saddle Lake. I speak Cree. In some areas I talk about spirituality.

I was looking at the television when the fourteen youths were killed in Montreal.[3] I watched the funerals. What a lovely church, I thought. All gold. And us we have, I go to this sweat lodge. Old humble rocks. We use water. And I just said that. It's just as good. It helps us just as much as if we went to a fancy church. I'm open-minded about it, okay? But why do we have so many religions? One is trying to top the other. One wants to be better than the other. They're all praying to the same Creator, Holy Spirit, Holy Father.

On Cree Heritage

My mother told me one day about her mother's family, and the next day about my father's family.[4]

You asked, did we talk about this? About losing treaty rights? You don't know. We were asked never to talk about Indian issues, treaty issues. You were not allowed to do this when we were young. We knew men who had asked questions, and they were taken off the Band List by the Indian Agent. That's how the government dealt with us in those years. We didn't stay silent, but we lived with these threats in our lives. How sad that is. We had some bigoted bureau-crats who were willing to threaten us that they would strip us from our own band membership.

[This problem with stripping us of our band membership,] it's not corrected yet. Especially in Alberta because there's oil and gas royalty rights here. In 1985 when Bill C-31 passed, across Canada the govern-ment had $100 million for housing for these women going back and living on reserves with their children. Not one red cent was applied in Alberta. The bands didn't apply for it. We were shunned. I'd like to say that one day, that very strong emotionalism that's there, it will be erased. And that they heal and start accepting that we are very few Indian people, both on-reserve and off-reserve, and that there are many, many white people.

Protecting Treaty Rights for all Generations

On September 29, 2008, Nellie Carlson spoke to the Eighth World Indigenous Women and Wellness Conference in Calgary, Alberta about the long struggle to end discrimination against women in Canada's Indian Act. She decided to tell her own story so that younger indigenous women would find courage to defend treaty and Aboriginal rights. When she returned home, she talked about her speech, and their response. Here is an excerpt from her reflections on that day.

NELLIE: I told them the history from the beginning. They turned and listened to me. You could hear a pin drop. Mary Simon[5] was the first speaker, and then I began to speak about how women had to make changes.

In 1950, I told them, I became very, very sick. This was twelve days after my mother's death. I was in the hospital with a ruptured appendix, and I almost died. I remember a doctor saying to my husband: "Had I known, Mr. Carlson, that you were willing to pay for the prescription, I could have given it to her." You see I had lost treaty rights, and the doctor thought he could not give me a prescription because I could not pay for it. I could have said to these young women, "We were the scapegoats of this nation at that time," but I didn't. Anyway, I said, I am going to stick to the *Indian Act* in what I am telling you.

I made up my mind on the bus down to Calgary what to tell these women.

A good doctor in St. Paul—his father was French, his mother Métis—he phoned the Indian Agent and suggested that they must reinstate my health care rights because I was so sick, and needed prescriptions. And if they agreed, I would have kept treaty rights for the rest of my life.

But the law changed again. The new law said that Indian
women who married non-Indians would lose their treaty rights.
Their children, too, would be taken off the band membership
lists. This made some women very angry. Philomena Deschamps
Ross had a son born in 1955. She wrote to her MPs to say that
he was a Cree band member in Hobbema, but he had lost treaty
rights, his oil royalty. She fought hard for her son's rights. His
name was Allan Ross. We called him Sonny. In 1967, he was reinstated along with 407 children, due to Philomena's hard work.

They turned quiet when I said that. I said to them: Our journey
along this trail was not for fame or anything. We were doing it for
our children's rights. That's it. Then I told them about Jeannette
Corbière Lavell and the *Canadian Bill of Rights* of 1960, about her
case. Somehow the government wanted Indian people to take this
issue to the Supreme Court of Canada, which they did.

I wanted to speak more openly in the speech about the Indian
men who had secretly supported us, and the Indian men who had
harassed us, and the treaty Indian women who refused to help us,
and the women's organizations that refused to help us. I wanted
to name all of these people. I held my tongue. I could have said
more. I decided to keep quiet on some things.

I told the women that certain native people did things the old
white man's way, meaning that they took the issue right off the
agenda. They couldn't talk about the ordeal because they needed
to protect certain women who had Indian status....So I told then
them how we went to Ottawa to support Jeannette Corbière Lavell
after her case went to the Supreme Court. When we got to Ottawa
we borrowed money from my son. My son gave us the money to
buy a train ticket with meals. In Ottawa, at the hotel, the phone
was ringing all night with harassing phone calls. We called the
hotel front desk, and said: "Shut off this ringing so we can sleep."
We were telling this white lady we met in the hotel this story
the next day. Her name was Hilda Cryderman. She gave us her

number. She was not married. She lived in the Chateau Laurier Hotel. She helped us to pay for our food, and other bills.

Margaret Hyndman also supported our work. This lawyer, Margaret, she helped us to get seats at the Supreme Court to hear the Lavell case. Someone phoned me at 6 A.M. "Nellie, Nellie get up!" they said. We got there at the court steps at 9.30. There were men who were swearing at us. Outright bitches, they said. That's how we were treated. We went into the Supreme Court with men swearing at us. I never mentioned that to the women in my speech. No. I just said that we were there for three days. I never mentioned that the government rented a plane for the Indian leaders to go to Montreal for a hockey game. I never did mention that.

Then I said, when the decision came down from the Supreme Court, the position was close, but it went against Jeannette five to four. We were disappointed! The Supreme Court Chief Justice Bora Laskin said it's up to Parliament to change this section, not the courts. Then I said: Here we go again! Bill C-47 was a Liberal Bill, a first try. Indian women and children would be brought into treaty, but grandchildren would be negotiable. It went through the House of Commons to the Senate. Charlie Watt, the Inuit senator, voted against it. That time we cried.

I told them how we went back to Ottawa, again and again, to ask for a change in the law, and how we talked to MPS and cabinet ministers and even the prime minister, Pierre Trudeau. And how Mary Two-Axe kicked me under the table for swearing out loud. Pierre Trudeau talked about the Constitution coming back. The Constitution would supersede the *Indian Act*, he said. We waited for many years after that for a change, but we never quit. We kept working.

I want those young people to know that Indian Rights for Indian Women, our organization, fought for their treaty rights. They forget that it was Jenny who wrote to the Human Rights Committee in Geneva, to the United Nations in New York, to everyone [to support Sandra Lovelace's appeal to the United

Nellie Carlson receives a Governor General's Award in Commemoration of the Persons Case in 1988 in recognition of her work to promote women's equality.

Nations for support]. Jenny explained the discrimination in those letters. That's when international organizations like the UN told Trudeau that if he wanted to be consistent to the agreements Canada had signed, this country would have to repeal Section 12(1)(b). They had no choice. Canada had just forgotten us.

And I kept speaking to these women.

I talked to them about dysfunctional families, and why that happened. I said the *Indian Act* really ruined us as a nation of people, and the residential schools did that too, because people like me were declared non-Indian. I am a proud Cree woman, I said. There were four hundred people in that room, and oh my God, I was right at home. I felt good. I was not even afraid. I said: My friend, Philomena Ross, died on April 7, 1985. She never got a chance to see that *Indian Act* changed, but it finally did.

Elmer Carlson and Nellie Carlson.

Bill C-31, it's not a perfect Bill, but so many people got their treaty rights back. I think of all of those women who were kicked off their reserves through the decades. Some ended up in Alberta's mental hospital, some as widows or raising children after marriage breakdowns, or seeing their children go to foster homes, all because so many people had no place to go. Many of their children have their treaty rights restored to them.

Oh, my goodness, when I stopped speaking, the people stood up and they clapped and whistled. I was so surprised.

I think they had not heard all of this before. I thanked them, and I thanked the organizers for inviting me to come there. I don't think they heard me say that. They clapped so long.

I think they were shocked. They had read a lot about the *Indian Act*, and the changes, but they didn't know the cost of it. Now they know. These First Nations and Métis women in the room, some of them, were doctors, lawyers and dentists. I think they are hearing this for the first time. This happened to women, I said. You have to know.

And so here we are now. It took us twenty-three years to work for this change, and another twenty-three years to talk about it to the crowd without emotionalism. We were not looking for fame, but just to get recognized as treaty Indians. We were looking to help our children. The government tried to persuade us that the women would be reinstated, and that would be the end of it. We wanted reinstatement of women and their children and their descendants. These issues have gone to court many times, in different provinces.

Bill c-31 is not perfect, as I said. It will rob our descendants. That is the most blatant abuse of treaty rights there can be. We know the bands are getting money from the federal government on a per capita basis, counting the Bill c-31 people on their Band Lists. We don't see any of that money. The people are not getting any benefit for it, people like us and our children. Yes, we're treaty Indian again, but on-reserve treaty rights are different than off-reserve treaty rights. When Bill c-31 passed, how much money was allotted for new housing for reinstated people in the cities? How much was spent on us? Not one penny. And most of us live off-reserve. Also this change in the law does not protect our descendants. In the future we will have full-blooded Indians who do not have treaty Indian status. So our struggle will continue, and the younger generation will have to pick up where we left off.

We never said we would write a book. Never. We just wanted to get rid of that Section 12(1)(b), and that's what we did.

 # Closing Words

I am thankful for the children for they will prosper. All the children who are sitting here hope that the Great Spirit will look down upon as one.

—ONCHAMINAHOS, CHIEF LITTLE HUNTER,
before signing Treaty Six at Fort Pitt, 1876

My Indian brothers, Indians of the plains, I have shaken hands with you. I shake hands with all of you in my heart. God has given us a good day. I trust his eye is upon us, and that what we will do will be for the benefit of his children.

—TREATY COMMISSIONER ALEXANDER MORRIS,
speaking to the Plains Cree before signing Treaty Six at Fort Carlton, 1876

FOR THE SAKE OF THE CHILDREN, Nellie Carlson and Kathleen Steinhauer have actively opposed sexual discrimination in the *Indian Act* for more than fifty years.

In 2009, the British Columbia Court of Appeal ruled in the Sharon McIvor case that the *Indian Act* membership rules continue to discriminate between men and women.

On March 11, 2010, the Government of Canada announced its intention to launch a new exploratory process on Indian registration, band membership and Aboriginal citizenship. Later that year, the government passed *The Gender Equity in Indian Registration Act*, and launched a consultation process with First Nations and Métis organizations in the opening months of 2011. Suggested topics to be examined include: emerging concepts of First Nations membership, citizenship and identity; residual discrimination and second generation cut-off; the current system of Indian registration under the *Indian Act*; First Nations' assertions of jurisdiction over citizenship, governance and identity; the relationship between programs and services and Indian status and band membership; and issues of unstated paternity.

In November 2010, Sharon McIvor petitioned the United Nations Human Rights Committee to investigate continuing gender discrimination in the *Indian Act*.

The Government of Canada continues to define who is a "registered Indian" and who is not. The struggle continues.

Family Tree

Ancestors and Descendants of
Nellie Carlson and Kathleen Steinhauer

Kinship Ties

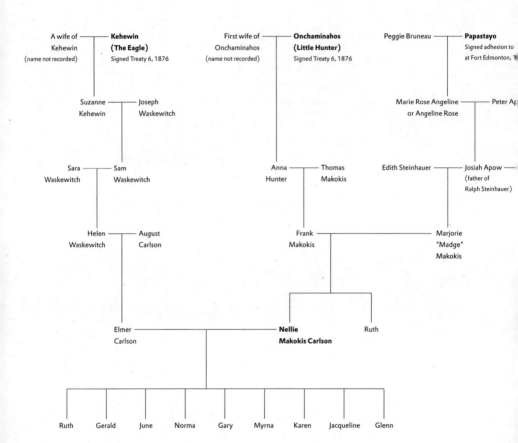

A wife of Kehewin (name not recorded) ——— **Kehewin (The Eagle)** Signed Treaty 6, 1876

First wife of Onchaminahos (name not recorded) ——— **Onchaminahos (Little Hunter)** Signed Treaty 6, 1876

Peggie Bruneau ——— **Papastayo** Signed adhesion to at Fort Edmonton, 1

Suzanne Kehewin ——— Joseph Waskewitch

Marie Rose Angeline or Angeline Rose ——— Peter Ap

Sara Waskewitch ——— Sam Waskewitch

Anna Hunter ——— Thomas Makokis

Edith Steinhauer ——— Josiah Apow (father of Ralph Steinhauer)

Helen Waskewitch ——— August Carlson

Frank Makokis ——— Marjorie "Madge" Makokis

Elmer Carlson ——— **Nellie Makokis Carlson** ——— Ruth

Ruth Gerald June Norma Gary Myrna Karen Jacqueline Glenn

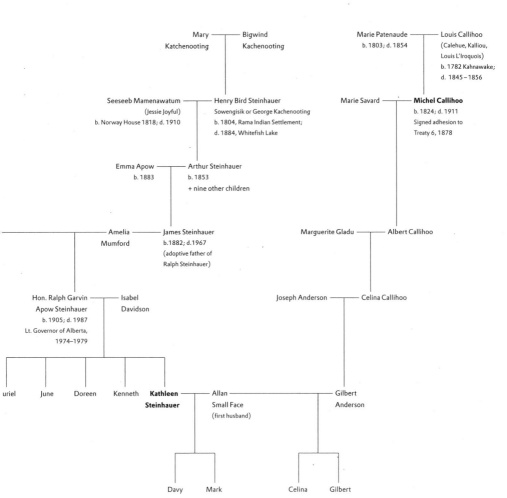

Timeline
Membership Rights and
First Nations Women in Canada

1869 The Canadian government defines the Indian reservation system within legislation.

1876 Canada introduces the *Indian Act* to govern every aspect of life on the reserves. The definition of Indian emphasized male lineage. An Indian was defined as any male person of Indian blood reputed to belong to a particular band; any child of such a person; and any woman lawfully married to such a person. If an Indian woman married a non-Indian, she lost her status but she did not necessarily lose her rights in practice.

1927 The *Indian Act* is amended to prevent anyone (Aboriginal or otherwise) from soliciting funds for Indian legal claims without a special licence from the Superintendent-General. This effectively prevented any First Nation from pursuing Aboriginal land claims, or any case of discrimination under the *Indian Act*.

1951 Amendments to the *Indian Act* established a government register of all Indian people, and defined those who were eligible to be described as "status" or "registered" Indians. From now on, only band members registered under the *Indian Act* had the legal right to live on-reserve, vote for band council and chief, share in band moneys, own or inherit property or be buried on the reserve.

Section 12(1)(b) stipulated that a woman who married a non-status man was not entitled to be registered. However, the wife or widow of a registered Indian man could claim Indian status, regardless of ethnic background. The "double mother" clause also stipulated that a person whose parents married on or after September 4, 1951 and whose mother and paternal grandmother had not been registered Indians before their marriages, would lose status and band membership on his or her twenty-first birthday.

In another amendment in 1951, registered Indian women—including non-Aboriginal women who gained Indian status through marriage—are allowed to vote in band elections for the first time.

1967 Mary Two-Axe Earley organizes a provincial organization, Equal Rights for Indian Women, in Quebec.

1967–1968 Jenny Shirt Margetts, Nellie Carlson, Kathleen Steinhauer and other women begin to meet to discuss discrimination against women in Section 12(1)(b) of the *Indian Act*.

1971 Jeannette Corbière Lavell, an Ojibwa woman born into the Wikwemikong band on Manitoulin Island, and living in Toronto, launches a lawsuit to reclaim Indian status. She claims Section 12(1)(b) of the *Indian Act* violates the equality clause in the 1960 *Canadian Bill of Rights*.

1971 Yvonne Bédard, born into the Six Nations Reserve in southern Ontario, brings a similar case to the Ontario courts.

1971 Women in Alberta who have lost their own treaty rights through marriage begin to organize their own campaign against *Indian Act* discrimination. After meeting Mary Two-Axe Earley, they found a national organization called Indian Rights for Indian Women.

1973 The Supreme Court of Canada rules against Lavell and Bédard in a narrow decision, finding that the *Canadian Bill of Rights* does not supersede the *Indian Act*.

1977 Sandra Lovelace, a Maliseet from Tobique, New Brunswick, files a complaint against Canada with the United Nations Human Rights Committee in Geneva, Switzerland. She had lost Indian status when she married, and wished to return to her reserve when the marriage ended. An articulate voice for the cause, she brings this discrimination to the Canadian public's attention.

1981 The United Nations Human Rights Committee finds Canada in breach of the *International Covenant on Civil and Political Rights* over discrimination against women in the *Indian Act*.

1982 The *Charter of Rights and Freedoms* becomes Canada's primary law. Section 35 states: "The existing Aboriginal and treaty rights of the Aboriginal peoples of Canada are hereby recognized and affirmed." However, Section 15 on equality rights will not come into force for three years in order to give the federal government and provinces time to bring their legislation in line with the *Charter*.

1984 Bill c-47, new legislation to amend the membership regulations affecting women in the *Indian Act*, gets first reading in the House of Commons. Eleven days later, it dies after a single vote in the Senate, cast by Inuit Senator Charlie Watt.

1985 On February 28, the Canadian government introduces Bill c-31, a Bill to eliminate sexual discrimination from the *Indian Act*, for first reading.

1985 In April the equality rights outlined in Section 15 of the *Canadian Charter of Rights and Freedoms* come into effect. Bill c-31 becomes law on June 28. These amendments to the *Indian Act* are intended to remove sexual discrimination, and restore status and memberships right for thousands of people, and increase First Nations local authority. However, the federal government maintains control over who is registered as an Indian, and the rights that flow from membership.

Women who have lost Indian status through marriage, and their children, can apply for reinstatement to a General List and a Band List. The reforms also allow non-status Aboriginal people whose families have lost status for various reasons to apply for registration based on their ancestry and lineage.

First Nations can determine their own membership rules and regulate who can live on the reserve. Also, under the new regulations, Indian status is terminated after two successive generations of intermarriage between Indians and non-Indians. In the future, a child will have to have at least two status Indian grandparents to claim Indian status.

1988 Nellie Carlson is the recipient of a Governor General's Award in Commemoration of the Persons Case to recognize her work to promote the equality of women.

1989 Sharon McIvor, a reinstated member of the Lower Nicola band in British Columbia, begins a court challenge of Bill C-31. She contends that the revised *Indian Act* still gives preferential treatment to people who trace their First Nations heritage paternally through their father's family rather than maternally through their mother's family.

1992 On June 11, the Royal Commission on Aboriginal Peoples holds a public hearing in Edmonton. In testimony before the commission, Nellie Carlson said: "Historically the *Indian Act* has thoroughly brainwashed us. Since 1869 an Indian woman already was legislated as to who she should be. Six times the *Indian Act* changed on Indian women. But each time she lost a little bit of her rights as an Indian."

1992 Kathleen Steinhauer launches a lawsuit in the Federal Court of Canada to be reinstated on the Band List of the Saddle Lake Cree Nation.

1995 Three First Nations in Alberta—Sawridge, Ermineskin and Tsuu T'ina—launch legal action against the Government of Canada to challenge the rights of band members reinstated under Bill C-31. They argue they have the right to determine their own membership. Their complex case is still before the courts.

1999 Kathleen Steinhauer wins her lawsuit and is reinstated as a member of the Saddle Lake Cree Nation.

2000 In the five years since Bill C-31 became law, 114,512 Canadians have gained Indian status while 44,199 applications have been denied. Women represent the majority of those who gain Indian status.

2005 The Native Women's Association of Canada and Quebec Native Women protest the continued sexual discrimination in the *Indian Act* in a demonstration on Parliament Hill in Ottawa as they mark the twentieth anniversary of Bill C-31.

2009 In April the British Columbia Court of Appeal rules in the case of *McIvor v Canada* that the *Indian Act* continues to discriminate between men and women in regard to registration.

2009 On November 6, the Supreme Court of Canada dismissed with costs the case of Sharon Donna McIvor against the Registrar of Indian and

Northern Affairs Canada, but the issue returns to the government for resolution.

2010 In March, the Government of Canada tables Bill C-3, *The Gender Equity in Indian Registration Act.* It announces its intention to begin a new exploratory process with First Nations and Métis organizations on Indian registration, band membership and Aboriginal citizenship. The Bill passes in December. From now on, eligible grandchildren of women who lost status after marriage will be entitled to Indian status. As a result of McIvor's legal challenge, another 45,000 people became eligible for registration.

2011 Sharon McIvor petitions the United Nations Human Rights Committee to investigate continuing gender discrimination in the registration rules of the *Indian Act.*

2012 Kathleen Steinhauer dies on March 4 at the age of eighty.

KATHLEEN STEINHAUER AND NELLIE CARLSON would like to honour all of
their colleagues in Indian Rights for Indian Women, as well as the movement's supporters in Alberta and across Canada. In particular, they would
like to pay tribute to the following people:

◆ The Activists of Indian Rights for Indian Women, and their Supporters

Jenny Shirt Margetts [Saddle Lake First Nation]: A founder of Indian Rights
    for Indian Women in Alberta, and a leader of the movement across
    Canada. Also an early advocate for Cree language education, and the
    innovator who brought the Awasis program to Edmonton's elementary
    schools.

Mary Two-Axe Earley [Kahnawake First Nation]: A founder of Equal Rights
    for Indian Women in Quebec, and a leader of the movement across
    Canada. In 1979, she was one of the first recipients of the Governor
    General's Award in Commemoration of the Persons Case, given to
    outstanding Canadian women. As the co-founder and vice-president of
    Indian Rights for Indian Women, she was recognized for "her tireless

efforts to ensure rights for native Indian women are equal to those of native Indian men."

Philomena Deschamps Ross: An early member of Indian Rights for Indian Women in Alberta who successfully challenged *Indian Act* discrimination against children disinherited from resource royalties on the Maskwachees reserve at Hobbema, Alberta. As a result of her efforts, 403 individuals were reinstated.

Mary Louise Frying Pan [Frog Lake First Nation]: a founding member of Indian Rights for Indian Women in Alberta.

Agnes Gendron [Cold Lake First Nation]: A determined member of Indian Rights for Indian Women who led twenty women to her band office on Treaty Day in 1995—for the tenth time in ten years—to demand the full benefits of reinstatement she had won through Bill c-31 a decade earlier. She was turned away, but told the chief she'd be back.

Hermine Anderson [Michel First Nation]: An elder who supported the Indian Rights for Indian Women movement in Alberta in its early years, and who travelled to Ottawa with its first delegation.

Veronica Morin: An Alberta elder who supported the Indian Rights for Indian Women movement in Alberta in its early years, and who travelled to Ottawa with its first delegation.

Marie Small Face Marule [Kainai Nation, Treaty Seven]: An educator and human rights activist who assisted Indian Rights for Indian Women in its early years. She later worked as executive director of the National Indian Brotherhood in Ottawa, and chief administrator of the World Council of Indigenous Peoples. More recently she has taught at the University of Lethbridge and has served as president of Red Crow Community College, a tribal college on the Kainai reserve.

Philomena Aulotte [Onion Lake First Nation]: A founding member of Indian Rights for Indian Women in Alberta, and a lifelong activist with the organization.

Frieda Patiel: An early member of Indian Rights for Indian Women.

Annie Collins: An early member of Indian Rights for Indian Women.

Caroline Wesley [Haida Nation]: A member of Indian Rights for Indian Women who worked for women's equality on the west coast of British Columbia, and for the restoration of Haida cultural traditions on Haida Gwaii.

◆ The Women who Launched Court Cases, and Appeals to International Human Rights Tribunals

Jeannette Corbière Lavell was born on the Wikwemikong Reserve on Manitoulin Island in northern Ontario. In 1970, Jeannette married David Lavell, a non-native man. Shortly after her marriage, she received a notice from the Department of Indian Affairs and Northern Development stating that she was no longer considered an Indian according to section 12(1)(b) of the *Indian Act*. Her lawsuit against the federal government reached the Supreme Court of Canada, along with Yvonne Bédard's case, in 1973. On August 27, 1973, the Supreme Court, in a majority of 5–4, held that the *Canadian Bill of Rights* did not apply to that section of the *Indian Act*, and dismissed both landmark cases. In 2009, Corbière Lavell became the president of the Native Women's Association of Canada, and continues to be an outspoken critic of the continuing problems in membership rules in the *Indian Act*.

Yvonne Bédard was born as a member of the Six Nations. In May 1964, she married a non-Indian, and had two children with him. She and her husband lived together off the reserve until they separated in 1970. She and her two children returned to the reserve to live in a house left to her by her mother, Carrie Williams. When she began to occupy the house on the reserve, the Six Nations Band Council passed a resolution ordering her to dispose of the property within the next six months. She took her case against discrimination in the *Indian Act* through the Ontario courts. On August 27, 1973, the Supreme Court, in a majority of 5–4, held that the *Canadian Bill of Rights* did not apply to that section of the *Indian Act*, and dismissed her case.

Sandra Lovelace is a Maliseet woman from the Tobique First Nation in New Brunswick who became known internationally in 1977 when she petitioned the United Nations Human Rights Committee over the mistreatment of Aboriginal women and children in Canada under the *Indian Act*. She is now a Senator representing New Brunswick in the upper house of the Canadian Parliament, where she continues to be an outspoken advocate of Aboriginal women's rights. She was named to the Order of Canada in 1990 in honour of her contributions.

Sharon Donna McIvor of Merritt, British Columbia, fought for twenty years to reinstate herself and her son, Charles Grismer, after she lost her Indian

133

status under the *Indian Act*. After she was reinstated, she launched a court challenge of Bill C-31, saying that the "second-generation cut-off" continued to discriminate against women. The British Columbia Court of Appeal found that the law continues to treat men and women differently, and the Government of Canada subsequently amended the *Indian Act* to conform to the ruling. Dissatisfied with what she considers a limited and inadequate response, McIvor petitioned the United Nations Human Rights Committee in November 2010 for a ruling on her allegation of continuing gender discrimination in the law. McIvor is a practising member of the Law Society of British Columbia, and a Professor of Aboriginal Law at Nicola Valley Institute of Technology.

◆ Supporters in the Community

Maria Campbell is a community activist, storyteller, writer, filmmaker and teacher whose best-selling memoir *Halfbreed*—an important document on racial relations in Canada—encouraged many First Nation people to become writers. She lived in Edmonton for a number of years, and became a close friend of both Kathleen Steinhauer and Nellie Carlson.

Muriel Stanley-Venne has been a Métis activist and community leader in Alberta for more than thirty years. A former vice-president of the Métis Nation of Alberta, she is also the founder of the Institute for the Advancement of Aboriginal Women, and the Esquao Awards for Aboriginal Women. In 2004, she won a National Aboriginal Achievement Award for Justice and Human Rights, and in 2005 she was named a Member of the Order of Canada.

Jim Robb is an Edmonton lawyer who worked for countless hours to represent and assist Indian Rights for Indian Women, first as a law student and later as the organization's legal counsel. He later became a law professor at the University of Alberta.

Jean McBean was an Alberta lawyer and social justice advocate who offered considerable time and energy to the Indian Rights for Indian Women movement. Born in in 1948, she practised law in Edmonton after 1973, both in private practice and as the first Senior Counsel of the Legal Aid Alberta Family Law Offices. She represented Kathleen Steinhauer in her legal challenge for reinstatement in the Saddle Lake Cree Nation. She died in Victoria, British Columba, in April 2012.

Dale Gibson was a Manitoba lawyer and legal scholar who returned from Harvard University to teach at the University of Manitoba in 1959. He moved to the University of Alberta in 1991 and taught in the Faculty of Law from until his retirement in 2001. While in Edmonton, he assisted Kathleen Steinhauer with her legal challenge for reinstatement.

Florence Bird was a Canadian broadcaster, journalist and Senator who chaired the Royal Commission on the Status of Women from its inception in February 1967. In a landmark report in 1970, commissioners recommended that the federal government end discrimination against women in the *Indian Act*. Bird died in 1998.

Margaret Hyndman was a feminist human rights lawyer, benefactor and advisor to Indian Rights for Indian Women. Called to the bar in 1926, she was the second woman in the Commonwealth to be appointed King's Counsel, in 1937. She died in 1991.

Thérèse Casgrain was an early feminist activist and CCF Member of Parliament from Quebec. She encouraged Mary Two-Axe Earley to take her campaign against *Indian Act* discrimination to the Royal Commission on the Status of Women. Later a Senator, she supported and advised Indian Rights for Indian Women in early lobbying efforts. She died in 1981.

Hilda Cryderman was active in women's rights at the provincial and national level for many years. Originally a teacher, she pioneered many programs in British Columbia schools then led the movement which resulted in the enactment of the province's *Equal Pay Act* of 1953. She befriended Indian Rights for Indian Women lobbyists in Ottawa and helped them pay expenses out of her own pocket. She was awarded the Order of Canada for her human rights work in 1985, shortly before her death in Vernon, British Columbia, in 1985.

Marguerite Ritchie was born in Edmonton in 1919, she became the first Canadian female lawyer named a federal Queen's Counsel in 1963. A Justice Department lawyer, Ritchie founded the non-profit Human Rights Institute of Canada in Ottawa. She was an outspoken supporter of Indian Rights for Indian Women in its early years when she worked in western Canada.

Nancy Ruth Jackman is now a Canadian Senator. The social activist and philanthropist offered financial assistance to Indian Rights for Indian Women for their lobbying campaign in Ottawa, and to support court challenges of the sexual discrimination in the *Indian Act*.

136

Introduction

1. The *Indian Act* is a federal statute enacted in 1876 by the Parliament of Canada under the provisions of Section 91 (24) of the *Constitution Act, 1867,* which gave Canada exclusive authority to legislate in relation to "Indians and Lands Reserved for Indians." Parliament has amended the legislation many times, but the version most relevant to this text is the *Indian Act ("An Act respecting Indians"),* R.S., 1951, C. 1-5. The statute continues to define who is an "Indian," and contains legal rights and legal restrictions for "registered Indians."

2. By 2011, the Department of Aboriginal Affairs and Northern Development estimated that more than 117,000 persons had regained or acquired "Indian status" as a result of Bill C-31 amendments to the *Indian Act* in 1985. The department estimates an additional 45,000 persons will be newly entitled to registration under amendments in Bill C-3, the *Gender Equity in Indian Registration Act,* enacted December 15, 2010.

3. The most recent census data in 2006 identifies almost 1.2 million Aboriginal people in Canada, of whom 53 per cent are First Nations citizens with registered status, 30 per cent are Métis and 11 per cent are

Inuit. Overall, the Aboriginal population represents four per cent of the Canadian population.

4. As of December 2010, the Indian Register listed 824,341 individuals with registered Indian status in Canada, including 108,318 in the province of Alberta. The number of registered Indians is expected to increase to 920,100 by 2026 according to government projections.

5. The United Nations Human Rights Committee is a tribunal of eighteen experts that now meets three times a year in New York and Geneva for four-week sessions. Among other activities, the tribunal examines individual petitions alleging violations of the *International Covenant on Civil and Political Rights* in countries around the world.

6. The *Canadian Bill of Rights* was a federal statute introduced by Prime Minister John Diefenbaker's government in 1960. It was a first try at human rights legislation but it was an ineffective remedy for Canadians who appealed an injustice to the courts. The *Canadian Charter of Rights and Freedoms*, entrenched in the Constitution, replaced it in practice in 1982.

7. Article 27 of the Covenant provides that persons "shall not be denied the right, in community with the other members of their group, to enjoy their own culture, to profess and practise their own religion, or to use their own language."

8. Bill, C-31, *An Act to Amend the Indian Act*, RSC, 1985, c I-5, was passed in June 1985, retroactive to April 17, 1985. It was intended to remove discrimination from the Act, restore rights to those who had lost them, and recognized First Nations control over band membership.

9. A leader of this long court fight was the late Walter Twinn, a chief of the Sawridge First Nation in Slave Lake, Alberta after 1966, and a Canadian Senator from 1990 until his death in 1997.

10. See Chapter Seven for a full explanation of the "second generation cut-off."

11. See the epilogue of this book, "Closing Words," and the Honour Roll for a detailed description of Sharon McIvor's legal challenge to Bill C-31, and her ongoing appeal to the United Nations Human Rights Committee.

Notes

1 Daughters of Saddle Lake

1. The Saddle Lake Cree Nation is the fifth-largest First Nation in Canada, with 9,300 members in 2010. To learn more about the Saddle Lake Cree Nation today, see their website: http://www.saddlelake.ca.

2. The Honourable Ralph G. Steinhauer [1905–1987], was a founder of the Indian Association of Alberta, and its president; a founding member of the Alberta Wheat Pool; a district president of the Farmer's Union; and a Liberal candidate in the 1963 federal election. He served on the band council of Saddle Lake Cree Nation for thirty-four years. For a detailed biographical sketch, see http://www.abheritage.ca/abpolitics/people/lt_steinhauer.html.

3. Treaty Day is an annual celebration of the signing of the treaty, marked by the ceremonial distribution of the five-dollar treaty payment to the members of the band. In the Cree culture, this is also a time of family visiting and reconnection with the community, a summer reunion. Nellie and Kathleen also refer to it later as "Treaty time."

4. The *Soldier Settlement Act of 1917* provided returning First World War veterans with free quarter-sections of land [160 acres] and $2,500 in interest-free loans. To do this, the federal government turned its back on a treaty promise in order to open up Indian reserve lands for white settlement, and exerted pressure on chiefs and band councils to sign land surrenders.

5. The Canadian government introduced regulations to the *Indian Act* as early as 1885 to outlaw certain Aboriginal ceremonies and traditions such as potlatches among the First Nations on the Pacific coast. Indian Agents on the prairies discouraged or banned the Sun Dance of the Plains peoples as the government wanted Aboriginal people to abandon traditional practices and adopt Christianity. This persecution expanded over time to include other ceremonial gatherings, including sweat lodges and pipe ceremonies. These ceremonies were often held in secret after that, and traditional spirituality went underground across the prairies, away from the eyes of the Indian Agent, but the ceremonies and beliefs did not disappear. The ban was lifted in 1951.

2   Surviving Residential School

1. The *Gradual Civilization Act* promoted assimilation in other ways. It set up a mandatory system of "enfranchisement" for Indian men who could read and write in English or French, had elementary education, had good moral character, and were free from debt. These men would receive fifty acres of land and be considered a regular British subject, but they would have to choose a surname approved by commissioners, and they would subsequently forfeit all rights and future claims to Indian lands, as would their descendants.

2. Kathleen's aunt, May Steinhauer, was a teenager at the time. She boarded at the Edmonton Residential School but attended classes in a regular Edmonton high school.

3. Maher Arar, a telecommunications engineer with dual Syrian and Canadian citizenship, received $10.5 million in compensation after the US falsely accused him of terrorism in 2002 and deported him to Syria where he was imprisoned and tortured.

4. Kathleen remembers one beating dislocated the hip of a bedwetter.

5. Dr. Chester Cunningham, founder and executive director of Native Counselling Services of Alberta. From 1970 to 1997, this agency grew from four court workers to more than 150 employees who served all of Alberta under his leadership.

6. Emma Minde published her own memoir as an elder: *kwayask ê-kê-pê-kiskinowâpahtihicik / Their Example Showed Me the Way: A Cree Woman's Life Shaped by Two Cultures*, told by Emma Minde, edited and translated by Freda Ahenakew and H.C. Wolfart (Edmonton: University of Alberta Press, 1997).

3   Love, Matrimony, and the *Indian Act*

1. Helen Waskewitch's father was Sam Waskewitch, once a chief at the Kehewin First Nation with a reserve located about 20 km south of the town of Bonnyville, Alberta. The First Nation is named for its founding leader, Kehewin, Helen's grandfather, who was chief until 1885 when the federal government removed him from office at the time of the Northwest Rebellion.

2. See the Introduction, "Two Strong Women Begin to Tell a Story" for a more detailed description of the Department of Indian Affairs' coloured tickets and their relationship to band membership.

3. The Charles Camsell Hospital opened in Edmonton in 1946 as a tuberculosis treatment hospital for First Nations, Métis and Inuit patients. Run by the Department of Indian Affairs and the federal Department of Health, it was also known as the "Indian hospital." The building was closed and abandoned in 1996, and now sits empty.

4. He wanted the Department of Indian Affairs to pay her substantial medical bill, and provide medications but due to her marriage to a non-status Indian she was no longer eligible.

5. The story of the court case is told later in Chapter Seven.

6. To learn about the Michel First Nation, see http://www.michelfirstnation.net.

7. For a full history of Louis Kwarakwante, Michel Callihoo and the Michel First Nation, see Elizabeth Macpherson's book, *The Sun Traveller: The Story of the Callihoos of Alberta* (St. Albert, Musée Heritage, 1998).

8. See the online exhibit, *Gilbert Anderson, Northern Alberta Métis Fiddler*, in the Virtual Museum of Canadian Traditional Music, http://www.fwalive.ualberta.ca.

9. Kathleen is survived by her children Mark Anderson, Celina Loyer, and Gilbert J. Anderson, and their spouses; as well as by her sisters Muriel Manywounds and Doreen Oke, and her brother Ken Steinhauer. Her son, Davy Small Face, her sister June, and two grandchildren predeceased her. At the time of her death Kathleen Steinhauer had eleven grandchildren and four great-grandchildren.

10. Pauline Gladstone was the daughter of James Gladstone [1887–1971], or Akay-na-muka, meaning Many Guns. He was the first status Indian to be appointed to the Canadian Senate. Cree by birth, he was adopted by the Kainai Blackfoot on the Blood reserve when he was born. In 1949, Gladstone was elected president of the Indian Association of Alberta and was sent to Ottawa three times to press for improvements to the *Indian Act*. The Gladstone family ran a large ranching operation on the reserve.

11. Hugh Dempsey, Canadian historian, author and Chief Curator Emeritus of the Glenbow Museum in Calgary, Alberta. Born in 1929, he has

written more than twenty books, focusing primarily on the history of people of the Blackfoot Confederacy. He married Pauline Gladstone in 1953.

12. For a biographical sketch of Marie Small Face Marule, see the Honour Roll at the end of this book.

13. Eugene Steinhauer [1928–1995] was a pioneer Cree broadcaster who toured First Nations communities in the late 1960s to interview and record elders, political leaders and others for a fifteen-minute radio broadcast. He was a founder of the Alberta Native Communications Society, and later a chief of Saddle Lake Cree Nation and a president of the Indian Association of Alberta. He led Alberta chiefs to London, England to oppose the patriation of the Canadian Constitution before treaty promises were honoured and protected, but he opposed the work of his female cousins in the Indian Rights for Indian Women movement.

14. Alex Janvier, a pioneer of contemporary Aboriginal art in Canada, is a member of the Cold Lake First Nation. Born in 1935 of Dene Suline and Saulteaux descent, he began to experiment with art as a child at Blue Quill's Residential School at Saddle Lake, and later received formal art training at the Alberta Institute of Technology and Art in Calgary, now the Alberta College of Art and Design, where he graduated in 1960. He helped bring together a group of First Nations artists, including Norval Morrisseau and Bill Reid, for a special exhibit at Expo 67 in Montreal. Described as the "first Canadian native modernist," he runs the Janvier Gallery with his family in Cold Lake.

15. Maria Campbell was born in 1940. For a biographical sketch of the Métis / community activist, author, storyteller and filmmaker, see the Honour Roll at the back of this book. Also see the profile in the *Encyclopedia of Saskatchewan*: http://esask.uregina.ca/entry/campbell_maria_1940-.html.

4   Indian Rights for Indian Women

1. Harold Cardinal [1945–2005] was an influential Cree political leader, writer, teacher, negotiator, scholar and lawyer. Born into the Sucker Creek Cree Nation in northern Alberta, he was elected president of the Indian Association of Alberta at the age of twenty-three, and led

the organization for nine terms. He was the author of two influential books, *The Unjust Society* and *The Rebirth of Canada's Indians*, and was a founder of the Prairie Treaty Nations Alliance in 1984. For a detailed profile, see the article, "Harold Cardinal," in http://www.thecanadianencyclopedia.com.

2. Stan Daniels, a well-known Métis activist with family origins in St. Paul des Métis, served several terms as president of the Métis Association of Alberta after 1967. He was an outspoken advocate for better housing and job opportunities for the Métis, and fair food prices in northern Alberta. His wife Christine [Whiskeyjack] Daniels was denied her membership in Saddle Lake Cree Nation when she married him—due to the discriminatory section in the *Indian Act*.

3. Harry Daniels [1940–2004] was a Métis activist in Saskatchewan and Alberta. He led the Native Council of Canada and was first president of the Métis National Council. He successfully argued for the specific recognition of the Métis in the *Constitution Act* of 1982.

4. Nellie quotes from the historical record. Duncan Campbell Scott, a senior civil servant and early Canadian poet, directed Canada's Department of Indian Affairs between 1913 and 1942. In 1920, under Scott's direction, it became mandatory for all native children between the ages of seven and fifteen to attend one of Canada's residential schools. Scott wrote: "I want to get rid of the Indian problem....I do not think as a matter of fact, that the country ought to continuously protect a class of people who are able to stand alone....Our objective is to continue until there is not a single Indian in Canada that has not been absorbed into the body politic, and there is no Indian question, and no Indian Department, that is the whole object of this Bill."

5. See the profile of Jeannette Corbière Lavell in the Honour Roll at the end of this book.

6. The National Indian Brotherhood organized in 1968 to represent treaty and status Indians across the country. It changed its name to the Assembly of First Nations in 1982.

7. Monica Turner of Geraldton, Ontario had married a Métis man, and lost her treaty rights.

8. A more formal organization, involving more people than they had attempted earlier.

9. The song "Squaws Along the Yukon," was recorded by Hank Thompson in 1958, with words and music by Cam Smith.

10. She has kept that clipping in her files, dated October 9, 1971.

11. Gordon Lee, an early treaty and Aboriginal rights researcher with the Indian Association of Alberta, is an elder at the Ermineskin Cree Nation in Hobbema, Alberta, and an acknowledged expert on the oral history of Treaty Six from the Cree perspective.

12. Ralph Bouvette, a leader and organizer at the Canadian Native Friendship Centre in Edmonton in the 1970s and 1980s, and well-known community worker in urban Aboriginal organizations.

5   A Tribute to Jenny Shirt Margetts

1. Descendants of the Cree band in the Edmonton area whose members signed an adhesion to Treaty Six at Fort Edmonton on August 21, 1877, and lost its reserve in south Edmonton.

2. Dr. Paul Davenport was president of the University of Alberta from 1989 until 1994.

6   How We Worked Together

1. Sandra Lovelace is a Wolastoqiyik or Maliseet activist and one of the best-known opponents of gender discrimination in the *Indian Act*. She received international recognition in 1979 for bringing her case against Section 12(1)(b) of the *Indian Act* to the United Nations Human Rights Committee. The first Aboriginal woman appointed to the Canadian Senate in 2005, she sits in the upper house as a Liberal. For a more detailed profile of this influential advocate for First Nations women and children see the Honour Roll at the back of this book.

2. George Manuel [1921–1989] led the National Indian Brotherhood from 1970 to 1976, and was a founder and early president of the World Council of Indigenous Peoples.

3. In 1969, fourteen University of Alberta law students created Student Legal Services of Edmonton to offer legal assistance to low-income residents in the Boyle Street District. Jim Robb and Jean McBean offered legal services and friendship to Indian Rights for Indian Women members for many years.

4. Marc Lalonde served as a senior Liberal cabinet minister in several portfolios under Prime Minister Pierre Trudeau, and was Minister of Energy
   at the time of this meeting.

5. Ovide Mercredi, a Cree lawyer from Manitoba, served as National Chief
   of the Assembly of First Nations from 1991 to 1997.

6. Willie Littlechild, a Cree lawyer from Alberta, was Member of Parliament
   for Wetaskiwin from 1988 to 1993. A member of the Ermineskin
   Cree Nation, he has also chaired an investigation of justice reform in
   Saskatchewan, and was named a commissioner in the Truth and
   Reconciliation Commission on residential schools in 2009. He has
   served as North American representative to the United Nations
   Permanent Forum on Indigenous Issues, and has been active in
   international human rights groups for Aboriginal peoples.

7. The new Constitution of Canada was proclaimed on April 17, 1982.
   With the *Charter of Rights and Freedoms* in place, the federal and provin-
   cials governments had two years to bring all legislation in line with
   the equality rights guarantees in the *Charter*. The Liberal government subsequently announced its intention to amend the *Indian Act* to
   remove gender discrimination against women.

8. Senator Charlie Watt was chief negotiator for the Inuit in the James Bay
   and Northern Quebec Agreement of 1975, which is considered the first
   modern-day treaty. A leader of the Inuit Tapirisat and Nunavik constitutional committee, he was appointed to the Canadian Senate in 1984.

7   Fighting for Our Birthright

1. Bill C-3, *Gender Equity in Indian Registration Act*, received Royal Assent
   on December 15, 2010. For a detailed description of this legislation,
   and its historical background, see "Legislative Summary of Bill C-3," by
   Mary C. Hurley and Tonina Simeone, Social Affairs Division, Library of
   Parliament. This report is available online.

2. Anne McLellan, then a law professor at the University of Alberta, later
   served four terms as a Liberal Member of Parliament for Edmonton
   Centre, from 1993 to 2006. She held several cabinet portfolios,
   including Minister of Justice and Deputy Prime Minister.

3. Don Mazankowski was a Conservative Member of Parliament for
   Vegreville from 1968 until 1993, and served as finance minister in the
   government led by Brian Mulroney.

4. Dr. Dale Gibson was a Manitoba lawyer and legal scholar who returned from Harvard University to teach at the University of Manitoba in 1959. He moved to the University of Alberta in 1991 and taught in the Faculty of Law until his retirement in 2001.

5. Walter Twinn, chief of the small but oil-rich Sawridge First Nation near Slave Lake in northern Alberta challenged the right of disinherited Sawridge members to reclaim membership after Bill c-31. Liz Poitras had launched a case for band membership after losing treaty status through marriage. The dispute was in the courts at the time.

6. Kathleen and her husband did not intend to move to Saddle Lake or claim housing or other local benefits of membership. The court case was therefore about principle, not financial gain.

7. Peter Lougheed, premier of Alberta from 1971 to 1985, had a Métis grandmother, Isabella Christine Hardisty, a member of a very prominent fur trading family with the Hudson's Bay Company in western Canada.

8. Kathleen believed that many people in Saddle Lake quietly understood the unfairness of excluding former members.

9. Joe P. Cardinal [1921–2004] was a war veteran who served two terms as chief of the Saddle Lake Cree Nation, and was widely respected for his community service as an elder working in corrections, health and education, advising young people in Cree traditional culture.

8   This Is Our Land

1. Over the years Nellie has been paid by Edmonton Public Schools and NorQuest College to work as a visiting elder with students of all ages. At the age of eighty-five, she still talks to NorQuest students every Wednesday and says they are very eager to learn about Cree culture.

2. Amiskwaciy Academy opened in Edmonton in 1999 as an innovative junior and senior high school with an emphasis on Aboriginal cultures, values, and ancestral knowledge and traditions. The school's name comes from the Cree word for the Beaver Hills, the traditional Cree territory around Edmonton.

3. Marc Lepine, a twenty-five-year-old man, murdered fourteen female engineering students and wounded ten women and four men in a gun rampage at École Polytechnique in Montreal in 1989. The funerals for the young women were broadcast on national television.

4. Nellie's mother spoke to her in a formal way about Cree traditional knowledge and family genealogy for two full days shortly before she died.

5. Mary Simon, president of Inuit Tapirlit Kanatami, a national organization representing Inuit peoples from all regions, was a senior Inuit negotiator during the Canadian constitutional discussions of the early 1980s. She later served as Canada's Ambassador for Circumpolar Affairs from 1994 to 2003.

Glossary

Terms Related to the Identity of
Aboriginal Peoples in Canada

Aboriginal Peoples: A collective name for the original inhabitants of North America and their descendants. Canada's *Constitution Act* of 1982 recognizes three distinct groups of Aboriginal people: Indians, now known as First Nations; Métis; and Inuit. More than one million people in Canada identified themselves as an Aboriginal in the 2006 census.

Bill C-31 Indian: An informal term or nickname, sometimes derogatory, used to refer to First Nations people who regained their registered Indian status after 1985 with the passage of Bill C-31, which includes amendments to the *Indian Act* that have removed some discriminatory clauses against women and their children. Between 1985 and 2005, the number of registered Indians in Canada more than doubled, in part due to this legislation.

blue-ticket holder: Before 1951, the Department of Indian Affairs used this term to describe Métis and non-status Indians, some of whom lived on reserves.

enfranchised Indian: First Nations citizens in Canada could not vote in federal elections before 1960, and confronted many other legal restrictions on their spiritual practices, right to appeal to the courts, purchase of property and alcohol, etc. for many decades. An "enfranchised Indian" is an archaic term used to describe individuals who either renounced registered Indian status to free themselves of these restrictions; or had their registered Indian status taken away from them when a government Indian Agent or the Department of Indian Affairs struck their names from a Band List or the General List without their permission or consent.

First Nations: The indigenous peoples of the territory that became Canada, people distinct from the Métis or Inuit, with treaty and Aboriginal rights recognized and protected in Canada's Constitution. The phrase First Nation in the singular usually refers to a single community, or sometimes a reserve belonging to that community. Canadians sometimes use the phrase informally to describe an indigenous person as a First Nations man or First Nations woman, but it is more common now for people to identify themselves by their specific tribal affiliation. The total population is nearly 700,000 people in 630 recognized First Nations.

Inuit: The indigenous peoples who inhabit the Arctic regions of Canada, Denmark, Russia and Alaska. The Inuit of Canada live in the territory of Nunavut; in the northern third of Quebec, in an area called Nunavik; in the coastal region of Labrador; and in various regions of the Northwest Territories. Canada's Constitution recognizes the legal and cultural rights of the Inuit as a distinctive group of Aboriginal people, separate from the First Nations and Métis.

Métis: A person who identifies as Métis, or claims ancestry in the Métis Nation, is distinct from other Aboriginal Peoples, and is accepted by the Métis Nation. The Métis emerged from the unions of First Nations women and European men in the fur trade in western North America before Canada became a nation. The subsequent intermarriages between Métis women and Métis men, who developed their own communities and culture, created a distinct Aboriginal people, whose rights are recognized in Canada's Constitution. The Métis National Council currently estimates a population of between 350,000 and 400,000.

nêhiyawak: The Cree people.

non-status Indian: The Government of Canada defines a non-status Indian as "an Indian person who is not registered as an Indian under the *Indian Act.*"

off-reserve: An informal phrase sometimes used to describe First Nations people who live in Canadian cities, towns or rural areas, and not on a reserve. First Nations tend to describe reserves as a permanent land base, claimed and guaranteed under treaty or Aboriginal rights; a home community for its membership. The Government of Canada defines a reserve as a "tract of land, the legal title to which is held by the Crown, set apart for the use and benefit of an Indian band."

red-ticket holder: Before 1951, the Department of Indian Affairs used the term "red-ticket holder" to refer to a woman with registered Indian status who had married a man without Indian status. In *Indian Act* amendments in 1951, the federal government denied these women and their children all treaty and Aboriginal rights.

registered Indian/status Indian: The Government of Canada continues to use the word "Indian" as a legal term to describe a First Nations person registered as an Indian under the legal definitions of the *Indian Act*, the federal legislation first passed in 1876 and amended many times since. Anyone whose name appears on the official Indian Register is considered a "status Indian" or a "treaty Indian," and is entitled to rights entrenched in Canada's Constitution. The names of these individuals can appear on a "General List" or a "Band List."

treaty Indian: The Government of Canada defines a treaty Indian as a "status Indian who belongs to a First Nation that signed a treaty with the Crown."

white-ticket holder: Before 1951, the Department of Indian Affairs used this term to describe an individual with legal Indian status.

Further Reading

Bayefsky, Anne R. "The Human Rights Committee and the Case of Sandra Lovelace." *Canadian Yearbook of International Law* 20 (1982): 244–66.

Bill C-31: Unity for our Grandchildren: Conference Proceedings, March 23–25, 1998, Ottawa Ontario. Ohsweken, ON: Native Women's Association of Canada, 1998.

Brown, Wayne. "Mary Two-Axe Earley: Crusader for Equal Rights for Aboriginal Women." *Electoral Insight*, (November 2003): 51–54.

Carter, Sarah and Patricia McCormack, eds. *Recollecting: Lives of Aboriginal Women of the Canadian Northwest and Borderlands.* Edmonton: Athabasca University Press, 2011.

Corbière Lavell, Jeannette, and D. Memee Lavell-Harvard, eds. *Until Our Hearts Are On the Ground: Aboriginal Mothering, Oppression, Resistance and Rebirth.* Toronto: Demeter Press, 2006.

Cruikshank, Julie. *Life Lived Like A Story: Life Stories of Three Yukon Native Elders.* Vancouver: University of British Columbia Press, 1990.

———. *Reading Voices: Oral and Written Interpretations of the Yukon's Past.* Vancouver, Douglas & McIntyre, 1991.

Green, Joyce. "Intersectionality and Authenticity: Exploring Identity and Citizenship." In "Exploring Identity and Citizenship: Aboriginal Women, Bill C-31 and the Sawridge Case," 197–244. PHD diss., University of Alberta, 1997.

Isaac, Thomas. "Case Commentary: Self-Government, Indian Women and their Rights of Reinstatement under the *Indian Act*. A comment on *Sawridge Band v Canada*." *Canadian Native Law Reporter* 4 (1995): 1–13.

Jamieson, Kathleen. *Indian Women and the Law in Canada: Citizens Minus.* Ottawa: Indian Rights for Indian Women and the Canadian Advisory Council on the Status of Women, 1978.

Lawrence, Bonita. "Gender, Race, and the Regulation of Native Identity in Canada and the United States: An Overview," *Hypatia* 18, no. 2 (2003): 3–31.

"Legislative Summary of Bill C-3: Gender Equity in Indian Registration Act," A Research Publication of the Library of Parliament, by Mary C. Hurley and Tonina Simeone, Social Affairs Division, 18 March 2010. Revised 15 November 2010. Publication Number 40-3-C3E. http://www.parl.gc.ca/Content/LOP/LegislativeSummaries/40/3/c3-e.pdf.

Leslie, John, and Ron Macguire, eds. *The Historical Development of the Indian Act.* 2nd ed., Ottawa: Department of Indian Affairs and Northern Development, 1983.

Miskimmin, Susanne E. "'You Can Always Give Back': Iroquoian and Algonquian Women's Construction of Identity." In Nobody Took the Indian Blood out of Me: An Analysis of Algonquian and Iroquoian Discourse Concerning Bill C-31, 66–98. PHD diss., University of Western Ontario, 1996.

Monture-Angus, Patricia. *Thunder in my Soul: A Mohawk Woman Speaks.* Halifax, NS: Fernwood Publishing, 1995.

Moss, Wendy. "Indigenous Self-Government in Canada and Sexual Equality Under the *Indian Act*: Resolving Conflicts Between Collective and Individual Rights." *Queen's Law Journal* 15, no. 2 (1990): 279–305.

Nahanee, Theresa. "Indian Women, Sex Equality and the *Charter*." In *Women and the Canadian State*, edited by Caroline Andrew and Sandra Rodgers, 89–103. Montreal: McGill-Queen's University Press, 1997.

154

Further Reading

Report of the Royal Commission on Aboriginal Peoples. "Urban
Perspectives." In *Perspectives and Realities*, 4: 519–621. Ottawa: Canada
Communications Group, 1996.

Report of the Royal Commission on Aboriginal Peoples. "Women's
Perspectives." In *Perspectives and Realities*, 4: 7–106. Ottawa: Canada
Communications Group, 1996.

Royal Commission on the Status of Women in Canada. *Report of the Royal
Commission on the Status of Women in Canada*. Ottawa: Information
Canada, 1970.

Sanders, D. "Indian status: A women's Issue or an Indian issue." *Canadian
Native Law Reporter* 30, no. 3 (1984): 30–39.

Silman, Janet. *Enough is Enough: Aboriginal Women Speak out*. Toronto: The
Women's Press, 1997. An oral history of the women's equality move-
ment on the Maliseet reserve in Tobique, New Brunswick, as told to
Silman.

UN General Assembly, *International Covenant on Civil and Political Rights*, 16
December 1966, United Nations, Treaty Series, vol. 999, p. 171, available at: http://www.unhcr.org/refworld/docid/3ae6b3aao.html [accessed
2 May 2012].

UN General Assembly, *Universal Declaration of Human Rights*, 10 December
1948, 217 A (III), available at: http://www.unhcr.org/refworld/
docid/3ae6b3712c.html [accessed 2 May 2012].

Wheeler, Winona. "Reflections on the Social Relations of Indigenous
Oral Histories." In *Walking a Tightrope: Aboriginal People and Their
Representations*, edited by Ute Lischke and David T. McNab, 189–214.
Waterloo, ON: Wilfrid Laurier University Press, 2005.

Whyte, John D. 1974. "The Lavell Case and Equality in Canada," *Queen's
Quarterly* 81, no. 1 (1974): 28–42. This article discusses the cases of
Jeannette Corbière Lavell and Yvonne Bédard.

◆ **Legal Documents**

*An Act to encourage the Gradual Civilization of the Indian Tribes in This
Province, and to Amend the Laws Respecting Indians*, SC, 1857 *[Gradual
Civilization Act]*.

An Act to ensure Fair Renumeration to Female Employees, BC 1953, c 6 *[Equal Pay Act]*.

Bill c-3, *Gender Equity in Indian Registration Act*, 3rd Sess, 40th Parl, 2010 (as passed by the House of Commons, 15 December, 2010).

British North America Act, 1867, 30–31 Vict, c 3 (UK).

Canadian Bill of Rights, SC, 1960, c 44.

Canadian Charter of Rights and Freedoms, being Part I of the *Constitution Act, 1982*.

The Constitution Act, 1982, being Schedule B to the *Canada Act 1982* (UK), 1982, c 11.

Gender Equity in Indian Registration Act, SC 2010, c 18.

Indian Act, An Act respecting Indians, RS 1951, c I-5.

Indian Act, An Act Respecting Indians, RSC 1985, c I-5.

McIvor v Canada (Registrar of Indian and Northern Affairs), 2009 BCCA 153.

Soldier Settlement Act, RSC, 1927, c 188.